GOOD DAYS

An A–Z of
Hope and Happiness

MICHAEL ROSEN

EBURY
PRESS

EBURY PRESS

UK | USA | Canada | Ireland | Australia
India | New Zealand | South Africa

Ebury Press is part of the Penguin Random House group of companies
whose addresses can be found at global.penguinrandomhouse.com

Penguin Random House UK
One Embassy Gardens, 8 Viaduct Gardens, London SW11 7BW

Penguin
Random House
UK

First published by Ebury Press in 2025

2

Typeset by seagulls.net

Printed and bound in Great Britain by Clays Ltd, Elcograf S.p.A.

The authorised representative in the EEA is Penguin Random House Ireland,
Morrison Chambers, 32 Nassau Street, Dublin D02 YH68.

A CIP catalogue record for this book is available from the British Library

ISBN 9781529148923

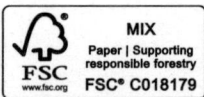

For Emma

Contents

Introduction

This is a book of days.

One way to make a book of days is to compile a book of interesting things that happened 'on this day' in any year. Robert Chambers made one like that in 1864. As he tells us, his book is full of the 'Oddities of Human Life' and the oddities are attached to the days of the year. You read a calendar of odd things that people have done. It's fun. A good way to spend some days, in fact. I hope you'll find that there are a good few oddities of human life in this book of days too.

My book of days is arranged differently, though: it is a book of what I think are good ways to spend my days, arranged in alphabetical order – what I've thought about and done which help me to have a good time. I've put these down as hints, reminders, tips and suggestions for how you might imitate, adapt or adopt some, any or many of these for yourself.

If at any time you think I sound as if I'm telling you what to do, then do please edit these out of your mind. At best, I'm just being enthusiastic. At worst, I confess, I'm showing my bossy side. Please forgive me by ignoring them.

So, to be clear: it's not a book of blueprints. It's not a guide. It's a book of what I hope are sparks and inspirations. As you read, I hope you'll find common ground, and think along the lines of 'I could give that a go', 'I could do something like that', or 'I used to do that; I could go back to doing it'.

I hope there'll be some surprises, jokes, echoes and resonances. When I read a book, I find that I get the most satisfaction if a book lights a blue touch paper, and I go off thinking, writing, researching, reading and doing. I hope that this book will work as a trigger for you.

But why?

It hardly needs saying but I'll say it anyway: we live in hard times. Things that some of us thought could and should have been solved, haven't been solved. Things that some of us thought would show signs of progress, haven't progressed. In many ways, wherever we look – locally, nationally or globally – there are things that have got worse. I don't need to list them. I know and you know that these things weigh on us. I was in a café recently and a man told me that he had struggled to get there up the Holloway Road – a long main road in north London. He then 'went off on one', a long diatribe about the hell that is the Holloway Road. He seemed particularly furious about the fact that though it's wide, it's slow. Unless this major moan was cheering him up, it did seem as if he was someone overwhelmed by 'now', 'where we're at', 'the way things are' and 'how everything's got worse'.

At that very moment, I was enjoying some lovely spicy green olives, my favourite lentil soup, hot falafel, mixed salad and freshly made Turkish bread. I know the Holloway Road. I once lived on it with my late-teenage sons (and half the time with my younger ones), at a time when things in my personal life were tough. I remember lovely late-night excursions with my teenage boys to a great kebab joint just over the road from where we were living. The Holloway Road sits in my mind as an oasis in a desert of troubles. And only a day before this chat in the café with my angry stranger, I had used the 43 bus that runs absurdly conveniently and directly from my house to a university theatre on the Holloway Road, where 350 children and I were celebrating the fortieth anniversary of the publication of the great *Journey to Jo'burg* with its wonderful author, Beverley Naidoo.

Why am I telling you all this? Because where that name 'Holloway Road' triggered annoyance and misery for my café man, for me it was, and still very much is, full of pleasure, delight and pride. I need such moments both in the here and now but also when I live amongst the memories, even though there is sadness, in that one of those teenage boys died.

So, I'm going to make a big claim: we can't do anything about the things that bring us down, if we are oppressed and depressed by them. We have to have hope. We need to be hopeful creatures in order to live. No matter how much events seem to point towards despair, telling us to be pessimistic, I think we have to find strategies and techniques to be hopeful. In spite of everything, we have to find reasons to go on. As someone once put it in a book, 'We can't go over it. We can't go under it. We've got to go through it.'

I can't make you feel hopeful. I can't guarantee you'll be happy. What I can do (and it's what I've tried to do) is tell some stories and give you some thoughts, which I hope, in themselves, will give you a moment of cheer. But more than that: as you will have guessed by now, I think that having moments of cheer is one of the ways we can have hope. Happiness and hope are linked.

So welcome to my book of days. Feel free to read it in any order you like, but I will point out that I've put my more general thoughts (dare I call them theories?) towards the beginning. As you read, you may well find me saying things like 'and that was a good way to spend a day', implying, 'why not try something like that yourself?' If you spot that I haven't said this, then please do go ahead – imagine I have written precisely that, and dabble with the idea of trying something like that yourself.

After all, what else can we do but share our experiences and ideas and hope that others will take them up and make them work for themselves?

A

is for Arouet

Who or what is Arouet?

Arouet is here right at the beginning of this book because it begins with A. But that 'A' is hidden behind three acts of disguise. A book appeared in Geneva in 1759, with a title that shows us the first two disguises. The title can be expressed in English as *Candide, or Optimism, translated from German by Dr Ralph*.

But it wasn't translated from German and there is no Dr Ralph.

The next disguise is to say, as indeed everyone does say, that *Candide* was written by Voltaire. It was as certain as it's possible to be certain that it was written by the person who called himself Voltaire, but Voltaire wasn't his name. His name was François-Marie Arouet.

Now, if you want to have a good day, right now, then please let me suggest that you spend a couple of hours reading *Candide*. Of course, I could recommend many different books but there's a particular reason for choosing this one by way of a starter for this book, and it's not just because the title promises 'optimism', which should surely be a place to start when thinking about your good day (although, as we'll see, it's a bit more complicated than that!). Yes, I think it's funny, clever and witty. I also think it's a wonderful, poignant satire and an eye-opener to ways in which people have deceived themselves (or tried to deceive others) about what to believe. It's also a book that has given us several phrases that are in every dictionary of quotations – like 'pour encourager les autres' ('to encourage the others') – a bitterly ironic phrase that can be said at a time of an execution: they chopped off his head 'to encourage the others'.

Or this one, which features more irony: 'I am the best man in the world, and yet I have already killed three men; and of these three, two were priests.'

Or this one: the reason why we use the phrase ironically 'this is the best of all possible worlds' is because one of the characters in the book, Pangloss, says in the midst of horrors and disasters: 'It is demonstrable ... that things cannot be otherwise than as they are; for things having been created for an end, all is necessarily for the best end.'

That represents the 'optimism' of the title (a philosophy belonging to the German polymath Leibnitz). Leibnitz put forward the idea that we live in the best of all possible worlds, a world created by an omnipotent, omniscient and benevolent God.

So *Candide* is not a tribute to optimism. If anything, it mocks optimism. And yet here's me giving you a book about 'good days' and I kick it off with recommending a book that seems to mock the very thought! What's going on?

Ah, but we haven't got to the last line of the book. I could put up a pretty good argument for saying that it's almost impossible to write about how to have good days, how to feel good about ourselves or feel good about life, without dealing with the idea that is in the famous last line of *Candide*. In French, it's 'Il faut cultiver notre jardin', which can translate as 'We should cultivate our garden' or 'We must cultivate our gardens' (though other versions are available, as we shall see!).

This is how the line appears: Pangloss has just given Candide a pompous little speech about how everything has worked out very well:

'There is a concatenation of events in this best of all possible worlds: for if you had not been kicked out of a magnificent castle for love of Miss Cunégonde: if you had not been put into the Inquisition: if you had not walked over America: if you had not stabbed the Baron: if you had not lost all your sheep from the fine country of El Dorado: you would not be here eating preserved citrons and pistachio-nuts.'

'All that is very well,' answered Candide, 'but let us cultivate our garden.'

[*Gutenberg translation*]

When I first read *Candide* 60 years ago, this came as a big surprise. After all, I had taken the book, right up to this last moment, as strong stuff, taking pot shots at people in power and the hypocrisy that keeps them in power. Pangloss is still wittering on right up to the very end about how everything works out for the best, even though we have seen that for millions of people it doesn't, and so we turn to Candide (who has been our witness to all that's wrong in the world) for some words of wisdom. And all he can offer us, I thought, are a few trite words about looking after your garden. Well, of course, it's not really Candide doing that. It's Voltaire getting him to say that, from within Candide's character, but positioning it as the last words of the book seemed to give the words some authority, the authority of the author, perhaps.

So, does Voltaire think that the way to be hopeful in life is to look after your garden? Or – another possibility – is he mocking Candide for being so limited, so narrow-minded as to think that the solution to all the awful things he's seen in life is to just look after your garden?

This is part of the infuriating delight of fiction. We can never know which of these two Voltaire intended, or indeed if he intended both at the same time, or neither! What we can do is speculate. (Please take that word 'speculate' as one of the pleasures of life and indeed one of the ways in which we can have 'good days'.)

So, let's do it.

At face value, Candide listens to what Pangloss has said and hears it as a summing up of the optimistic philosophy which, from his experience, he knows is rubbish. So he counterposes something. Instead of nodding sagely as yet another disaster comes over the horizon, comforting oneself with the thought that it's all working out OK in the end, we should do something. But what? What can we do? Let's ask ourselves that question. We might say that we can try to save the world. We might say that we can do good things to others and for others (the New Testament seems to say that that's what we should do and Voltaire would have been very aware of that philosophy). Or we can lower our sights and say to ourselves, we can only do what we can do 'on our patch'.

Let's be literal. Though it's quite rare to hear anyone offer the cultivation of your garden as a philosophy for saving the world, or curing society's ills, you do hear people talking of the joy and relief they get from growing things. My father was one. He spent thousands of hours pottering in his garden, prodding the earth, going to garden centres and choosing plants – and, just as important, I think – talking to people (even me) about cotoneasters, myrtle bushes and *Polyspora axillaris*, otherwise known as the 'fried egg plant' (not a fried eggplant, though). He was, in a way, and for some of the time in his life, a walking embodiment of the last line of *Candide*.

But what if it's more metaphorical than that? What if it doesn't actually mean 'do your garden' but means more like 'do your own thing', or 'sort out what's under your nose' or the like? I guess we are all familiar with people who are (or who think they are) very good at sorting out other people's lives but are pretty hopeless at sorting out themselves. You could put up a good argument for saying that for as long as we trust the kind of people who screw up other people's lives, we will never solve anything. The terrifying stories of what has happened in cults has often come about as a consequence of people entrusting themselves to nasty maniacs. That's an extreme and obvious example. Much nearer to home are the situations in which we've been obliged to obey someone or we've accepted some-one who tells us how to behave, but then, further down the line, we've found out that they have been corrupt, hypocritical or have committed the very same 'crimes' that they condemned. Shakespeare spotted that 400 years ago in *King Lear* when King Lear himself says:

> *Thou rascal beadle, hold thy bloody hand!*
> *Why dost thou lash that whore? Strip thine own back.*
> *Thou hotly lusts to use her in that kind*
> *For which thou whip'st her. The usurer hangs the cozener.*

Just to unpack that: Lear is imagining talking to a 'beadle' (a court usher) saying that he is guilty of lusting after the whore and yet that's what he is whipping her for. In a similar fashion, the usurer punishes the cheat at a time when usury was seen as a form of cheating. So, trying to sort out, or rule over, other people's lives without sorting out your own, solves nothing.

Now back to the garden. Was Voltaire saying, if you're doing your own thing, at least you're not being hypocritical, you're not exploiting others, stealing from others, being brutal or unkind to others? Is that what Voltaire meant? And, further, if everyone just got on and did their own thing, the world would be a better place. Would that work?

We know one problem with it: a lot of what you put in the garden or use to make the garden comes from the hard, low-paid work of others (seeds, lawnmowers, spades, trowels, fertiliser). Refuse collectors come to pick up the garden waste. To fetch what we need, we use vehicles and power. In other words, even when we think we are only doing our own thing, we connect with 'society'. We can't all simply or only do our garden. A lot of the people making it possible for us to do our garden may not have the luxury of being able to do their own thing.

Did Voltaire know that? Was he mocking Candide for being naively selfish, thinking that the solution to the awful things in the world was to be found in tending his garden, and that the same applies to all of us? Or maybe Voltaire didn't have a solution. Maybe he didn't have any more of a solution than his character, Candide. That last line of the book is, then, a challenge to anyone thinking that they have anything interesting or useful to say about how to live in this world.

So let's take up that challenge: if it's mindlessly optimistic (like Pangloss), then we not only delude ourselves, but we become cruel in thinking that people's suffering is for the benefit of others. If we turn in on ourselves and think we are solving the problems of the world by telling everyone to do their own thing, we delude ourselves into thinking that our own personal peace of mind is a remedy for everything. However (and there's bound to be a 'however', isn't there?), it's hard, damned hard, to do anything useful or helpful if you can't find ways to have that peace of mind. I think that's what my father thought. He found peace of mind in his garden, which enabled him to do the good things (often for others) that he wanted to do. But then you can turn that on its head and say instead, maybe one way to have peace of mind is to do things that are useful and helpful.

By the way, one of the reasons we get ourselves into knots about things like 'am I doing this for me or am I doing this for others?' is that we have, built-in to us, a view of 'me'. We think of 'me' as someone 'I' make. We watch hundreds of movies, read hundreds of books, hear politicians talking as if we are each self-made beings. The truth of it, though, is that the 'me' is created *with* others. We arrive in a world that is already made and being made – by others. Others talk to us, play with us, educate us, employ us and the 'me' thinks back, talks back, plays back, discovers, investigates, makes decisions out of all these millions of interactions *with* others. We make each other as we make ourselves. Stuff happens; we respond. As we respond, we change. As we change, we change others. Though we divide ourselves into 'individuals' and 'society', or into 'me' and 'others', the truth is that there is no fixed border between myself and other people. Even the language we use that we might think of as personal is made up of words that have been used before by others.

Four hundred years ago, John Donne wrote:

No man is an island, entire of itself; every man is a piece of the continent, a part of the main; if a clod be washed away by the sea, Europe is the less, as well as if a promontory were, as well as if a manor of thy friends or of thine own were; any man's death diminishes me, because I am involved in mankind; and therefore never send to know for whom the bell tolls; it tolls for thee.

[*modernised spelling*]

Do we have any reason to think that Voltaire might have been thinking about something beyond 'do your own thing'? Candide talks of 'our' garden. But what is 'our garden'? One story tells how once the whole of humanity had a garden – the

Garden of Eden. Then, the story goes on to say, humanity screwed up, and, as the Bible tells us, we got a lot of pain and suffering as a result. Voltaire was a 'deist'. He believed that God existed, made the world and left us to work out what to do with it. The book *Candide* can be taken as a view of how humanity is screwing up, not getting things right. Not yet.

One more interpretation of that last sentence then: what if Voltaire meant the 'garden' of the Earth? We must cultivate (look after?) the Earth and all who live on it. Is there a way of thinking about that last sentence as if it were speaking back at the disasters and horrors we meet earlier in the book, saying that they happened because we weren't looking after *our* garden? The garden that belongs to *us*. So, this way, it's a plea to not accept the horrors we've met earlier, and it's not a selfish plea to do 'my' thing but it's more of a plea to do 'our' thing – together.

I find that thought helpful and hopeful. Helpful, hopeful thoughts don't come along very often, so we should grab them when they do. And hang onto them, don't you think?

SUGGESTION

As this book is both thoughtful (in the sense of 'full of thoughts') and practical, here comes the practical bit: why not read *Candide*?

B

is for Bad Days and Bannisters

It may seem strange that the second entry in a book called *Good Days* is 'Bad Days'. Perhaps it should fall foul of trade description law.

Hang on in there, there's a reason.

But first, let's deal with 'days'. What's with 'days'? I'm inspired by two pieces of writing: one by the poet Philip Larkin and the other by the singer-songwriter Sheryl Crow. Larkin wrote, 'Days are where we live.' Sheryl Crow wrote, 'Every day is a winding road.' They each had a bit more to say about days, but let's stick with the idea of a day. What is it and why might it be useful to think of it in the context of this book?

By 'day', I don't mean the formal matter of 24 hours, and I don't really mean a day to include – as it does technically – the time we're asleep. The day I'm talking about is that conscious period of time between our major sleeps. Like Larkin, I'm of the view that this 'day' is where and how we live. We live 'day by day', 'taking one day at a time', 'living from day to day'. You may have heard it said that for most people, the longest series of numbers we can remember easily without making any special effort is seven. Yes, for some people it's fewer and some people can easily remember more. And with effort, practice and repetition most of us reach longer numbers, as with our mobile phone numbers. That said, there seems to be some kind of average, ordinary length that we can manage without much effort. I think of a 'day' as something like that.

This is how it works: a day marks a period of time in which you can do stuff. Most of us make the day-between-sleep when we do our eating, peeing and pooing – the basic stuff of life. Yes, some of us have to get up in the night and 'take a leak' (as my son puts it). Some of us also wake in the small hours and 'get the munchies' (as another one of my children puts it), but by and large we do most of that stuff in that day period. That's the basics.

Then there's whatever we mean by work. By definition, we do work when we're awake and the times when we're asleep mark the boundaries for it. Obvious. But this imposes a pattern on what's possible – whether that's imposed by employers or by your own routines as self-employed. You know that if you push it too hard, there'll be problems the next day. If you mess about, 'bunk off', give up – again, there'll be problems the next day. If you're retired, there can be other problems – days can be empty and, we might say, 'meaningless'. There doesn't seem to be very much 'to do'.

Even the idea of 'days off' and the 'weekend' are part of this routine of days, the 'diurnal' as it's called. The idea of TGIF (or TFIF), the idea of the 'Saturday night', the way we think of some activities as being more suitable for a Saturday rather than a Sunday – all have their roots in the diurnal, with the old matter of sabbaths and worship running along underneath.

But what about emotions and feelings? Is there a way in which these are part of this idea that 'days are where we live'? One way to think of feelings is that they run to and fro across time – past, present and future – as with memories from the past, reactions to events in a day, and then all the emotions involved in thinking forwards about the future: what might happen, what could happen, what we're afraid might happen, what we hope will happen and all the attendant feelings that go with these fantasies.

Our thoughts break out of the capsule of the day by going back into memories and forwards into possible happenings, but my argument here is that we live those emotions in the now, in the day itself. There's nowhere else to live them. We go through the acts of remembering (past) and thinking ahead (future) in the reality of the now. The now is in the day. In that sense, even our mental life is in the day.

And there's a limit on these thoughts. That's to say, we can't think them forever. As for me, I find that it's not possible to stick with one train of thought for much longer than an hour or two. Admittedly, we can come back to that train later in the day, and indeed tomorrow, the day after, the day after that, but of course, each time we do that, in reality, it'll be different. It'll be at least as different as a film we watch for the second or third time and probably more different because it's us who are, in a sense, making the film. It's our train of thought that we're making, so we can remake it, change it, develop it, revise it, how we want. But again, I'm going to claim that the place where these trains of thought live is in a day.

When we wake up, there's a sense of us 'starting again' or 'giving that thought another go' in the time available – which will be in the day or part of the day. Days are our chapters.

What else does Philip Larkin say about days? He says:

They come, they wake us
Time and time over.

This reminds us that we don't control days. Our diurnal existence is controlled by the rotation of the earth and our need for sleep – some combination of both, perhaps. By the way,

I'm not denying the lives of millions (billions?) of people who choose to or have to work at night. As I said, this 'day' I'm talking about is the 'time between sleeps'. I'm not talking about 'daytime' or 'nighttime'.

Larkin's line 'time and time over' reminds us that not only do we live *in* days but when we think ahead, we often think ahead to a day or days. That's where our life will go on: the day we're going to get married, the day I'm going to meet my old friend, the day when I have my operation, the day when I do my exam. Quite often, if it's an 'event' we plan a day around the event: how we're going to get there, where we're going to eat, what we might do afterwards, how we'll get home – and hundreds of variations on that. So days are where we live and days are what we imagine coming up ahead.

Then Larkin says:

They are to be happy in:
Where can we live but days?

Well, 'they are to be happy in' is what I'm trying to write about in the rest of this book, so I'll leave that to one side for the moment. The question 'Where can we live but days?' is what I've been discussing so far in this chapter. Sleeping is obviously some kind of life, some kind of existence, but not the existence I'm talking about! Yes, there isn't anywhere else to live but in days.

Now Larkin's poem takes a twist. He writes:

Ah, solving that question
Brings the priest and the doctor
In their long coats
Running over the fields.

In his own poetic style, we know here that he's talking about religion, medicine, death and the afterlife, but it's pretty clear that he wants to shelve all that. It's not what he's talking about. He talks of 'solving the question' by way of not solving the question! And I'm happy to join Larkin in that. I'll come back to it when we meet my daughter telling me what kind of human being I am – as daughters do.

Now what does Sheryl Crow tell us?

She tell us: 'Every day is a winding road.'

SUGGESTION

As an experiment, you can try writing a line that begins 'Every day is …'

We're led to believe from the words in the song that the line doesn't come from Crow herself, but was one said by a 'vending machine repair man' with whom Crow was hitching a ride. It doesn't matter if it's the man's line or Crow's but it's a nice expression of how our way of life – our work, how we live – often shapes how we see the world. If you're driving about on the long distances of the USA between one broken vending machine and another, then indeed every day *is* a winding road. But of course, there are other senses to it too. As we go through a day, it winds around places, people, events, feelings. It's a good metaphor. It shows us how, if we're lucky enough to be active in our thoughts and bodies, we move. And that little phrase 'every day' reminds us, yet again, that these movements of mind and body happen in the day, day after day.

But Crow has more to say about days. She says that the days in her song are when anything goes and she talks of each day being a faded sign.

The first of these suggests (as do other parts of the song) that the persona singing is 'going along with' what's happening, perhaps being on the road with this vending machine repair man. The great advantage of travel is that the day appears to unroll for you. You don't have to make the effort to roll it out through your own actions and thoughts.

The second (the one about the sign) suggests something different. Along the side of road there are always faded signs. A day might be marked or even described by one faded sign after another. I once wrote a poem about the faded signs I saw on the road between Tucson and Phoenix in Arizona and, by doing that, it told a story of past times in that part of America. But there's another way in which our days are, as I've suggested, full of the faded signs of our own lives. We go through a day with fragments of our past life coming up on our mental TV screen. Our minds are full of 'faded signs'. They come to us, as Crow says, 'every day'.

As you might guess, I love this song!

But Crow hits another tone. In the song she wonders why she feels alone and, again, why she's a stranger in her own life.

As if she isn't puzzled enough by these thoughts, she also wonders if everything she's seen was real – did everything really happen?

So what seemed a bit like a road movie, an adventure, a carefree friendship (a romance?), a matter of just seeing what goes, now touches on a note of loneliness and dislocation, alienation, of not knowing who she is. Why has this adventure turned into something where she's not sure about whether anything is real, even herself, because she might be a stranger in her own life?

This kind of speculation has run through lyric poetry for hundreds of years, but what's interesting about it on this theme of 'days' is that it takes place deliberately and consciously contained in a song about the meaning of 'what-is-a-day?' The home of this alienation in this song is in the day, the kind of day that this vending machine repair man is going on, down that winding road and/or on the winding road in Crow's mind.

This train of thought brings us to 'bad days', like the ones in the title of this essay. Crow says in the song that sometimes you're 'high' and sometimes you're 'low'. That's a feature of days. So my thought here – and perhaps it's a very ordinary thought – is that one of the ways we make good days, is thinking up ways to avoid bad days. That is, we make good days by making days not bad, or less bad. Perhaps that's really, really obvious because if you're down, you're not up. If things are going badly, they're not going well. But that's not all there is to it. We humans are thinking, reflective, speculating, responding beings. If we think things are going badly (or might go badly), that brings in the question of what can we do about it? What do we know about ourselves and our situation that can trigger in us a tactic or an approach that can make the bad stuff not-so-bad?

I hope that the rest of the book will talk about this.

Oh yes, and bannisters. Stairs are the most dangerous thing you meet in your life every day. You meet other dangerous things often, occasionally or even regularly for a while, but not every day throughout your life (unless you stay indoors in a bungalow every day, though).

Stairs are lethal.

The best way to make them less lethal is to hold the bannister. I once posted this on social media and the response was immediate and immense. Horror stories came in straight away of accidents, disasters, breaks, long convalescences, changed lives, permanent injuries and – sad to say – even deaths.

SUGGESTION

You want to avoid having a bad day? Hold the bannister. Well, you could do that literally, or even turn it into a statement about life! Maybe there's a Sheryl Crow song in that.

> *I was once coming down the stairs*
> *on a day that started out as a fail*
> *And there was an old guy there*
> *who called out, 'Grab the rail!'...*

You can write the rest! (Or any other lyrics along this line, for a version of your own!)

C

is for Curiosity

I once came home from secondary school with a message. I said to my father, 'Our RE teacher told us that Jesus said, "Be meek."' Quick bit of background: my father was a Jewish atheist who had just reluctantly left the Communist Party. No surprise then, he wasn't having it. 'Be meek?' he said. 'Be meek?' (He said nearly everything twice.) 'Why would you want to be meek?'

To be absolutely honest, I'm not sure that at the time I knew what 'meek' meant. It wasn't a word I ever used and, come to think of it, it wasn't a word that I had ever heard outside of RE lessons with Miss Mount. (That really was her name. No laughing at the back, please.)

So, I didn't have an answer to the question 'Why would you want to be meek?' but then I was too arrogant to ask what it meant. We had already got past the matter of the meaning of 'meek'.

Instead, I sat and waited for him to tell me why there was no point in being meek. I was often in that situation of sitting and waiting for my dad to go on. One way in which my father took the matter of parenting very, very seriously was to give my brother and me lectures. He seemed to have a vast, inexhaustible resource of 'stuff' in his head, and any random question could suddenly open the sluice gates and out it would gush. I could already sense that this thing about being 'meek' was going to be one of these sluice-gate moments. And the thing about a sluice-gate moment is that first you got the 'stuff' on the word in question, and then you got the follow-up. It was like that person who says they're going to make a pie and finds that they've got some pastry left over and says, 'Oh well, I might as well make some jam tarts ...'

And that's what happened.

First, he told me what was wrong with 'meek'. He said it was giving in to people, apologising for yourself, when probably inside you didn't feel meek anyway. So you would be stifling yourself.

In the back of my mind, there was Miss Mount, also talking about 'turning the other cheek' (again, no laughing at the back, please).

So, 'meek' was bad. Sorted.

Now next up, was the leftover pastry: the jam tarts.

He had an alternative to 'be meek'. He said: 'Be bold.' Now, I did have some idea of what 'bold' means. Knights of old were bold; brave people in history books were bold. They 'did something bold', which nearly always meant doing something in a battle. But out of sight there was another 'bold' which mothers and grandmothers said to us kids. It was a local word for 'cheeky'. 'Don't be bold.'

My father explained that he didn't mean either of those. He meant that if you believed in something, then say it or do it. Don't apologise. Just go ahead. I think it was a kind of 'who dares, wins' strategy. He wanted my brother and me to try things, take risks, go for it.

So, there you are, that was his reply to Miss Mount.

But he wasn't finished. He had dealt with the binary 'don't be meek, be bold', but now he was going to move out of the box. He had another 'be something' for me: 'be curious'.

One of the curious things about the word 'curious' is that it can go in two directions. If you say someone is curious it can mean either that they are curious about things in the world, or that they are a person who invites other people to be curious about them. In other words, it either goes outwards or inwards. So it can mean 'inquiring' or 'strange'.

Which one did my father mean?

He meant inquiring. Even so, it's been my experience since I was about six years old that people have found me curious. I can remember a time when the photographer had come to school and taken photos of us children. For some reason, when I was in 'first year juniors' (now Year 3), Miss Howlett (that was her real name) decided to make a pile of the photos at the front of the class and hold them up one at a time. As she held them up, we called out the names: 'John Hill' (real name) – we all shouted, 'John Hill!'; 'Diana Waller' (real name) – 'Diana Waller!', 'Malcolm Budd' (real name), and so on: 'Brian Harrison' (real name), 'Geoffrey Latimer' (real name), 'Valerie Bean' (real name), 'Carolyn Acaster' (real name) … You may have guessed from this that there is something oddly obsessive about me making this list. In the hunt for good days, one of the strangely satisfying things I do is run through the names of people in my classes from when I was very, very young. There's a serious reason for this. If we lose who we were, there is a way of thinking that this is a way of not knowing ourselves. It means we've lost where we come from, part of what has made us.

Anyway, back with the photos. (I get there in the end.) Miss Howlett (I told you that was her real name, didn't I?) is holding up the photos. We're calling out the names. Then it gets to me. She opens up the crisp card folder and holds up the photo of me. And then, amazingly, incredibly, people don't call out my name; they laugh. They point at the picture and laugh and laugh and laugh.

Why?

To be absolutely honest, I don't know. I have the photo. I look at it. To me, it looks like a cheery little chap, a little bit tousled, perhaps. A little bit freckly. Perhaps the collar is a bit loose. The tie is perhaps not tied perfectly but it's not hysterically funny. I really can't see that it's a reason for a whole class to burst out laughing and then ... carry on laughing!

So, as I was saying. I was curious.

But also as I was saying, it wasn't what my dad meant. My dad meant be curious about everything. Go about the world inquiring. Don't accept what they chuck at you. If something happens, find out stuff about it. I think the implication here was that if you find out loads and loads of stuff, you could be like him and so when someone looked into the distance and said, 'I wonder what kind of cloud that is' or 'what was that play that Shakespeare wrote about the guy who was really, really jealous?' you could dive in and tell them.

It really was built into my father and lasted for the whole of his life. One of the last conversations I had with him, he was telling me to read a book he had just read. He was 89 and very ill but he wanted to know more about the life of someone whose ideas he admired and, get this, he wanted me to read the book too.

But let me go back to catching the Curiosity Bug from my father (and from my mother too, actually).

Part of the way my parents thought about progress in life was to go camping. What? Why did they believe in camping? Why did they insist that 'the boys' (my brother and me) had to do this? Well, as a kid, I figured that it was connected to all the other lefty things they did. Was it in one of those musty books on their shelves? Perhaps in Karl Marx's *Das Kapital*, it said, 'You must go camping'?

And perhaps there was an extra bit, some kind of footnote, in *Das Kapital*, where it said, 'When you go camping, go somewhere where it rains a lot.' So that's why we constantly ended up on the Welsh Borders or the North York Moors, where it rained every day for five weeks. Then one year, our parents said, 'We're going to France'. And I thought, *Great. It's going to be baking hot all day every day.* We went to the Jura Mountains and it rained every day, and it rained every night. It rained non-stop for five weeks; my dad dug trenches round the tents but even so there was a river that ran through my tent and I got dysentery.

But I think my parents thought it was doing us good. Wet sleeping bags – doing us good. A river flowing through the tent – doing us good.

In the mornings, my father would remember his time in the American Army (he was an American citizen). The first thing we'd hear, in the middle of Yorkshire, would be my father shouting in a voice that sounded like an old US film star like John Wayne, 'Hey, youse guys! Shit, shine, shave and shower!'

And walking. They were in love with walking. As if it wasn't hard enough to get out of a tent into Welsh drizzle, they had this idea that we should head out along paths, through woods, over hills. My father would have the map and say to my mother, 'Look here, Con, there's a tumulus.' What?! What's a tumulus???

Sure enough, after about five hours of trudging through the drizzle, my father would stop and say, 'There! The tumulus.' And in a field next to the road was a lump. Something you would never notice. A round heap, covered in grass. I looked at it. Is this what we came for? The old man was still excited: 'A tumulus!' It didn't get much more thrilling than that, eh? Weeks later, my brother, in the bedroom, rucks up the blankets, puts on his Dad voice, and says, 'Look boys, it's a tumulus!'

But hey! Before I get too distant, contemptuous of this even, scroll through another 30 years, and I'm standing in a barn in the middle of the English countryside, with my two sons aged about 12 and 8, and I'm pointing at the ceiling. I'm just about to say, 'How extraordinary the beams and rafters are

...' and my younger son puts on his Dad voice (that's me, of course) and says, 'Extraordinary, look at the beams, boys! They could be at least 500 years old.' Or as my step-daughter once said on one of these occasions, 'You know, Dad, just because something's old, doesn't mean it's good.'

But it's no use. They didn't cure me of it. I am a believer in being curious.

If you're in the countryside in France in the summer, there's a very good chance you'll come across a hornet. Or, to be more precise, a hornet will come across you. One way a hornet will find you is in the evening. A lone hornet will appear out of a nearby wood and come for you like a Chinook helicopter, piloted by someone who thinks you're a terrorist. You duck, it flies on and hits a nearby vertical surface, window, wall, beam, car door ... If that surface is in any way edible, the Chinook turns into *Tyrannosaurus rex* and starts biting. You don't have to see it. You hear it munching. If this happens just the once, you may think, 'That's life. That's what happens in hot countries.'

But it may well be that if you're in the same spot at the same time, the next day, the whole thing happens all over again. Maybe there's a slight alteration in the geography. Someone has left a window open, and the Chinook flies straight through the window and hits a beam, and again, as before, it starts chewing on the beam. You can hear it from outside on the terrace: 'Pkkkrrrh! Pkkkrrrrh! Pkkkrrrh!'

Now again, if you want, you can just shrug and put it in that part of your head that says, 'Weird but ultimately boring.' Or, if you're anything like me, you might wonder, what the heck is going on? What are hornets? Why would this happen? Is it me? Do French hornets think I'm a terrorist? Or is there some reason for what's going on, insofar as anything in life and the universe has a reason? (A serious question, by the way – see G for God.)

Don't worry, I'm going to keep this brief, but what I found out about hornets is that every so often hornet colonies produce a female. This female heads off from the nest to go off to start up another colony. They fly till they reach a potential place to start and do what they're equipped to do, which is chew holes in organic material so they can hunker down and start laying eggs. Or something like that.

Why do I always try to dig further into things I'm curious about? The fundamental reason is because I don't want to be a passive victim of what the world throws at me. I don't want to be only and purely a receiver. I want to be a reactor, a responder. I don't want to feel as if I live in an incomprehensible world that dominates me. I don't want to feel that the world is any more mysterious beyond what has to be mysterious, but I love the idea that one of the best ways to 'receive' the world is to approach it with curiosity.

One more example. As you may know, one of my children died. He died of complications from a meningitis infection. It was the most bewildering, devastating thing that has ever happened to me. It felt senseless, absurd and cruel. For a time, I thought that it was as if something or someone had done it 'to' me. At that moment, I was a victim. It wasn't only senseless in itself but it also made me feel that I was helpless. I couldn't put meningitis on trial. I couldn't kick meningitis. This was a hopeless, helpless hole to be in. One thing I did was put 'be curious' into action.

At the time, I didn't know what meningitis is, I didn't know how it behaves when it's inside humans. So I was curious about it. I studied meningitis. I'm by no means an expert on meningitis, but the main thing I found out was that what had happened to Eddie wasn't some weird, senseless act of hate against me, it was something very, very normal: a bacterium multiplied in his blood. It's what happens. We live with bacteria and viruses. They're out there. They get into us. We have ways of dealing with some of it, a lot of the time. Sometimes these ways don't work.

I've written and talked about this many times, as in my book *Getting Better* (apologies if you've read it before). It's here in how to have a good day because one of the great enemies of being able to have a good day is, of course, being overwhelmed by the death of Eddie. So what I'm saying here is that if I can turn to a place, a resource that can keep that overwhelming feeling at bay, then so much the better. In my case, it's that knowledge about bacteria, viruses and human beings. For you, it might be something quite different, but all the same:

Be curious.

SUGGESTIONS

Here some ideas to pique your own curiosity:

- Watch your cat for half an hour and ask yourself why they are doing what they're doing. (There are many internet sites that have explanations.)

- Ask yourself what is the best opening line of any book, poem or play in the world.

- What is the space–time continuum?

- If there is life on another planet somewhere in the universe, how would we communicate with it?

- Can the history of the world be explained in terms of one group of people thinking that they're better than another group of people?

- What's the last book you didn't read?

- Does anyone know you?

- What do elephants think about?

- Why is your street named the way it's named?

- Why don't we still die of 'the plague'?

D

is for Death

Preamble: you came to this book thinking it was about good days, so what's death got to do with it? Surely death is the end of all days, good or bad. Yes, but it's my view that one way to have good days is to sort out in our minds what we think about death. So rather than poking it away under your old jumpers in the bottom of the wardrobe, it's better to get it out and shake it all about. In fact, I find that as and when I make peace with death, it gives me the strength to better appreciate my days.

Some thoughts: death has a way of spoiling things. Our problem as human beings is that we like attachment – or if you prefer a different word – 'love'. We lap up attachment when we're very young and we go looking for it for the rest of our lives. We may or may not be good at giving it. But wherever we are in this world of attachments, we can be pretty sure that if the person we love or get love from, or even want love from without getting it, dies, then we feel terrible. That's grief. And grief can last for a short time, a long time, or forever – in the sense that it lasts for as long as we're alive. As I say, if you're in the hunt for good days, this may get in the way. We may feel that it's not possible to have a good day now, tomorrow or ever.

That's death of the 'other'. As if this wasn't enough to be bothered about, there's also another death to bother about – our own. At first glance, the death of others and our own death are miles apart, but I'm far from being the first person to say that when we feel deeply about someone else's death, we also look upon the face of our own death. And vice versa, when we look on our own death, we think of the death of others. Our problem, as you'll know, is that though we can look upon other people's deaths, we can't look on our own, unless we create fiction, fantasy and ghost stories.

One of the most powerful and graphic ways this has been presented to us is in Dickens's *A Christmas Carol*, when a ghost makes it possible for Scrooge to see how the world will take it when he dies.

Scrooge says to the ghost, 'You are about to show me shadows of the things that have not happened, but will happen in the time before us ...'

If you don't know what happens, I'll tell you: it's not good.

As we read on, we discover that someone has died, and when businessmen speak of this person, one says, 'It's likely to be a very cheap funeral ... for upon my life I don't know of anybody to go to it.'

So this person is friendless.

Later, we discover that people have stolen this person's last belongings to sell them to a 'fence', including, even, a fine shirt that he was going to be buried in – a shirt that someone has dressed the corpse with.

'Somebody was fool enough to do it, but I took it off again,' says one, before adding, '[h]e can't look uglier than he did in that one.'

By now, we realise that this dead person is Scrooge and we are looking at this scene through Scrooge's eyes. We see and hear his horror.

With this device, Dickens collapses into one image the death of the other and the death of ourselves. He makes us think about something which is essentially absurd: what would we think if we heard that people despised and mocked us so much, and were so contemptuous of us, that they would strip a garment off our dead body and sell it?

(I say 'absurd', meaning it's absurd for anyone – I'm one of them – who thinks that death means the end of consciousness and awareness of anything, for, after all, people such as myself believe that we won't know anything after we've died.)

Now here's my point: I think that in a way, every time we hear of someone's death, read an obituary, go to a funeral, listen to the speeches, have a chat about someone who's died, at least one part of us is thinking about our own death, posing to ourselves many versions of the question: 'How will others talk of me when I die?'

When Scrooge contemplates this – and the death through poverty of the infant Tiny Tim – it becomes a route for redemption: he decides to become a better person, with the suggestion that if others thought like the redeemed Scrooge, society itself would improve. Good days, indeed!

But where does this leave me and you, grieving and bereft, full of regrets, miseries, if-onlys, and that sense of a loss of an 'attachment', a loss of love?

I can't speak of the comfort that people take from believing in an afterlife, a deity, or any kind of supernatural force at work, overseeing this. I'm someone who believes there is only us. This life is all we have. However, before I go on, there are complications to that view of things. For a start, the life we live has from the outset something of the lives of others in it, through our genetic make-up. And then when we die, there is a material way in which the atoms of our body don't disappear – they carry on in new forms. Then, speaking 'metaphysically', we carry on in the minds of those who knew us. If we leave behind artefacts, some people may keep those too.

Even so, as far as I understand life and death, I don't see much difference between me and a dandelion or a butterfly. Reproduction produces us; we have various life-forms; we die.

I understand that, for some, this is a profoundly depressing thought. But can I turn that feeling on its head? If this is all we are and this is all we have, then this suggests to me that we have to pay attention to the fact that we are no different from other humans – a fact that up until now, most of the people who have ever ruled over us have ignored. But more than this: it suggests that we are not separate from dandelions and butterflies but that we are in some kind of chain or 'continuum' with them.

Digression: my daughter came home from university and said, 'Dad, you are an optimistic nihilist.'

I said, 'Am I?' To tell the truth, I knew the meaning of the two words 'optimistic' and 'nihilist' but I didn't know what they meant if you stick them together.

'Yes,' she said, 'because you don't believe that there's anything outside of us, no gods or anything, so you think we should make the most of the life we've got.'

'Yes,' I said, thinking, *Ah, so that's why we agreed with you that it would be a good idea for you to go to university … so you would come up with thoughts like that.*

So, why the optimism? Why the 'optimistic' glued to the 'nihilism'?

If there's no afterlife, if there are no gods arranging things, if this is all we've got, then there isn't much point in being miserable. Further, we should try not to make other people miserable and, if anything, when we can, we should try to help make other people be not-miserable.

There's another point about being miserable. If you're miserable, it's very hard to do anything. If you don't do anything, you become even more miserable. Now I'm someone who thinks life is pointless. That's to say, I don't believe that I'm here or you're here or any of us are here for any kind of purpose beyond that of our own lives. This tells me that though life is pointless, the only point there can be to life is make this life as worthwhile as possible. That said, there's no point in making it worthwhile for me, while making it not worthwhile for others. So if the point of life is for it be worthwhile, the chances are today will turn out good – if you do something worthwhile. On the other hand, if you're miserable, the chances are that you not only won't do anything worthwhile, you won't do anything, full stop. You might see where I'm going with this: I'm making a connection between Doing and Feeling Good.

I haven't always known all this and, when I've known it, I haven't always believed it, and even when I've known it and believed it, I haven't always known how to put it into practice. It's possible I don't know how to do it even now. Maybe it's an objective to pursue rather than something that is simply done.

I can say, then, that if I think of death as this finite end (with the provisos that I gave before), then I find it easier to think of now, this day, this time here, as being the 'all we have', the time we have to get on and do whatever it is that we think is worth doing. Because, sure as anything, I couldn't do it before I was born and I'm not going to be able to do it after I've died.

But what about the loved one who's died? How could they have been so selfish to have not waited till we went first? Believe it or not, there were moments after my son Eddie died that I not only thought 'it' was cruel that he died but I also that 'he' had been cruel to have died!

One of my main reasons for regret and sadness is that I feel cut off from conversations with him, *about* him. One of the things we do with people we know well (and especially with family members) is play the 'do you remember when …?' game. (It's a great way to have a good day.) Together, we go over memorable moments, we write and rewrite history together. If there are moments any of us have to be sorry about or sorry for, we can try to heal something; if there are gaps we want to fill, things that weren't said – and much more – we can give it a go. Sometimes we 'get told' by others, telling us what we should or should not have done, what we could or should have done better. It's all part of how we make ourselves and go on making ourselves. We do it through making and remaking histories together. If someone dies, these come to a stop. You are stuck in the buffers and can't go on having these conversations. Instead, the conversations become frozen, sometimes in places you wish they weren't frozen.

One way round this is to have conversations with others who knew the person who's gone. These can be hard. My son had a life of his own. He was nearly 19. He had several lives that were quite separate from each other: his last years at school, his time with the mates that he played sport with, his workmates in the theatre (he was a 'crewman' in the West End), his girlfriend and of course the life he had with me and the family. I have to admit with huge regret that I know very, very little about all the parts of his life apart from the one with the family.

Over time, I sometimes imagine, he would have told me things about these 'other' parts of his life, just as I shared with my parents the lives I had away from them. Before Eddie died, I was trying to be a good dad by leaving him to live those other lives without my being a busybody. Because he died when he did, I didn't find out. But there are groups of people, alive now, who did know him. What should I do about that sense that there are these gaps, where Eddie was his own man? Should I dig out the people he was with and ask them what they thought of him, what stuff they got up to?

For years, I haven't done anything about it, if those people didn't come to me. Then, not long before writing this, I did some digging. I asked myself, 'What became of Greg?' (not his real name). I remember Eddie talking about Greg as his best mate. And here we are, 25 years since Eddie died and I haven't exchanged a single word with Greg. Or with Harry or Rob or Ned or Josh or … (not their real names). At this point, I feel an ache. It's as though I haven't been fair to Eddie, that I haven't bothered to find out who he was becoming, where he was at, how he had become so much more than being just the person in our family.

What would you do? Would you get in touch with one or some of them? I decided to. I'm just beginning. I've made a start. I've started to hear bits and pieces about Eddie that I had no idea existed. I started to hear some things that have made me proud of him (even more proud than I was anyway!). In fact, meeting up with Greg for a couple of hours in a pub not far from where we sat with Eddie just over 25 years before was a good day! At times painful, but a good day all the same.

Another thought: whether someone is alive or dead, the past has gone. When I sit in a state of regret and loss about Eddie as a child, I can (if I let it) be a place only and purely of regret and loss. It's as if I say to myself, 'That funny moment when Eddie found a dead mouse and thought it was a gerbil is sad because Eddie isn't here any more.' Why do I do that? Why do I spoil that funny moment by smothering it with Eddie's death? After all, that moment is no more 'gone' than the scenes with any of my other children or the scenes with my father or mother or brother. They are all 'gone'. So, I tell myself, I shouldn't taint these fun memories with Eddie with the fact that he's died.

I can tell you, it's taken some time to think that one through! So this is a way of pulling memories of Eddie into the good days.

I can also say that thinking about this helps me think about what it means to die. I can live with the paradox that I think life is purposeless by keeping focus on this day today in which I'll have a go at doing something worthwhile.

SUGGESTION

Think of a good day you had with someone who died. Really focus on it. Get into it. Be there in your mind. See if you can remember the smells, the texture of people's clothes, the look on people's faces, the weather, the shape of the furniture or the buildings, the noises and sounds, your thoughts at that moment. Try to push away the feelings of regret or loss or remorse or anger. Just concentrate on that one moment. Live it. Whatever that moment was is what life is. If you colour it or flavour it with the feelings you've had since, we lose sight of what it was at the time. You can 'do' the flavours another time! This is about being 'in' that moment.

E

is for Experiment

Here's the scene: I've arrived at a college in Oxford – Wadham College. It's 1965, or maybe 1966. In a kind of back garden, two students are standing about 30 or 40 metres apart. They're doing something that I had never seen before but I'm guessing anyone reading this has seen by now: they were throwing a Frisbee to and fro between each other. I'm not going to claim that this is the first Frisbee ever to be seen in the UK – far from it – but it really was the first one I had ever seen. It turned out that one of the students had been to the US and bought it there.

Like small kids who watch while people on a beach seem to be having a great time, playing volleyball or cricket, I found myself staring and staring, wanting to have a go. There's something deliciously attractive about the sight of someone launching a Frisbee into the air, seeing it swerve and hover and, if the people are good at catching it, watching them pluck it out of the air as if it's been gently passed to them by a kindly but invisible hand.

But even as I thought how magical it all was, a recollection came to me. My parents were not authoritarian but they did have a sense that my brother and I ought to 'help out'. It came from their politics. They thought that a family was like a boat and everyone had to do something to keep it going. They even had a semi-ironic phrase they'd chant – 'all for the collective' – as a way of coaxing my brother and I to do the shopping, tidy our rooms, sand down a sideboard that needed to be painted and .... of course ... always ... do the washing up. Oh no, please, not the washing up. Yes, even the greasy pans.

At home, my brother and I often ended up turning it into one of those scenes we had seen at the circus when the clowns walk into each other's wet mops, stand in buckets and end up throwing water in each other's faces. Our version would involve using bicycle pumps as giant water pistols, bottles of washing-up liquid as squirters, and bicycle rain capes as shields. There was also something disgusting that my brother did with the egg cup in which my father used to mix mustard powder and water. My brother still finds it funny 70 years later.

But what about those long camping holidays? Yes, long camping holidays with three meals a day, cooked on 'Primus stoves' and open fires, and eaten off lightweight aluminium plates. Once again, my brother and I were recruited to step up and 'do the washing up for the collective'. But here, there was a whole other dynamic: we were outside, in a field, with a stack of lightweight plates. You can guess what we discovered – nay, invented: we could spin the plates into the air and across the campsite. Doing the washing up spread and lengthened into an Olympic sport, hurling, catching, measuring distances, scoring points and, of course, arguing.

I don't want to make a huge fuss about this (I do, actually) but in essence my brother and I, and the boys we used to camp with, invented the Frisbee on the Welsh borders, near Skenfrith, in 1955. Well, I say that, but you will have noticed that what we didn't do was patent it, or go to a manufacturer and produce any. Something else you can notice with a tiny bit of research is find out who really did invent the Frisbee and indeed why it was called a 'Frisbee'. And I'm pleased to say, the story is in its own way very similar to the one I've just told you about us spinning aluminium plates.

And I mentioned clowns earlier. I can't be the first person to suspect that clowns and jugglers invented Frisbee-like spinning and chucking centuries ago, long before the first Frisbees. Even so, I don't want to take the gloss off those lovely campsite games with the aluminium plates.

Now I want to pull out some observations about this. What did we actually do? At some point one of us must have experimented with spinning and chucking a plate. Maybe we had seen a clown do it. I remember going to Olympia with my mum to see the Bertram Mills Circus in about 1952 and weeping with laughter at the clowns. Perhaps I was the one who applied what I had seen to the new circumstances of our campsite washing-up chores. Or, more likely, it was my very scientifically minded brother who, as I remember, would work out exactly how to get a pillow to land on my head from his side of the bedroom by applying 'parabolic theory', or so he said.

So on the campsite we start to throw plates. We try out different kinds of spin, different angles of hand for when the plate leaves the hand, different angles of arm as the hand pulls back and hurtles forward before the release, the best grip for holding, the best wrist movement for imparting spin, the best grip for the moment of release. All this involves experiment, talk, discussion, observation, proof, adaptation, conclusions, revisions and so on.

In this tiny bit of mucking about – in what is a fleeting, trivial moment in my life – is the essence of what it means to experiment and invent. A set of processes, ways of thinking, ways of acting, ways of learning that lie at the heart of many of the great leaps in science, the arts and technology.

Well, this book isn't about experimenting to find out the best way to get to the moon. It's about how to have a good day. What I'm claiming here is that one way to have a good day is to take part in some way or another in this process of experimenting.

Perhaps I've picked an extreme example to kick off with. In terms of children's pleasure, I've chosen a high-end moment. Not all experiments can hit these heights. No matter – it's the principle I'm on about here. I'm talking about any kind of experiment, no matter how trivial, how small. Why? Because to experiment is to do something new, it's to discover something in the world around us, it's to discover something about yourself. And a big discovery (or it may be a reminder) is that we don't have to be passive receivers of what the world throws at us. We can take any part of the world and experiment with it, see what happens if …

Now let's take all this down a peg or two. The scene: it's ten o'clock at night. I should be closing down. Not looking at a screen. Not thinking about tomorrow. Not eating or drinking.

Then I remember that in the freezer is the tub of Belgian chocolate ice cream I bought the other day. I say to myself, 'This is silly. You don't *neeeeeeeed* a bowl of Belgian chocolate ice cream. You don't need scoops of Belgian chocolate ice cream, sitting in a crisp white bowl. You don't need to taste shavings of Belgian chocolate ice cream sitting on your tongue, melting slowly and slipping down your throat. You so, so, so don't need Belgian chocolate ice cream.'

For some mysterious reason I then discover that I have found my way into the kitchen. How did that happen? A few seconds ago, I was in the living room. Now I'm in the kitchen. Inexplicable. And very surprisingly, I'm standing next to the fridge. Dear old fridge. There you are, your doors and drawer holding in the substance of life, our basic needs. And Belgian chocolate ice cream. I wonder how it's getting along these days. I don't suppose we have any. I'll just check.

I open the freezer drawer. Oh my poor little Belgian chocolate ice cream tub, all on its own in the freezer basket. I suppose the offspring have been at it. I'd better take a look just to see whether that's what they're up to these days. A kind of fatherly, medical check.

Oh my, it looks to me as if there are about four spoonfuls left. The problem is we don't have any spoons. Oh, we do!

Now, let me break the flow here.

So far, so ordinary, you might think. Haven't we all done a ten o'clock trip to the fridge to see what might be there? Maybe not all, but I'll massage myself with the thought that quite a few of us do this. It can certainly cap a day, turning it from ordinary to good. But this entry is about Experimenting. Surely there's no experimenting left to do. I have the tub. I have the spoon. I don't even need a bowl. It's a done deal. Just get on with it.

Ah but …

It's at this moment, my experimenting mind turns on. What if (and that's the key phrase in the world history and practice of experimenting) … *what if* I were to add something to the Belgian chocolate ice cream? That old roast potato that's sitting in the fridge? Belgian chocolate and cold roast potato? Maybe not. What about smearing it with hummus? No, hummus can wait. What about … raisins?

Now you're talking. What is it about ice cream makers that hardly any of them seem to have discovered raisins? They can stuff ice cream full of cookie dough, little itty bits of chocolate, mint, salt (what? why?), and even that Ben and Jerry thing 'Phish Food', which I can never separate in my mind from the word 'pish' (Yiddish for pee). But raisins? Well, not in any ice cream in my local supermarket freezer cabinet.

But, my experimenting mind says, why don't I rearrange the known world, and add raisins to these last four scoops of Belgian chocolate ice cream?

I go to the dried fruit cupboard. You may think I'm joking here but Dad and his dried fruit hoard is both a fact and a family joke. I have turned a family tradition (my mother prescribed dried fruit throughout my childhood) into an obsession. I keep myself constantly equipped with dried figs, dates, cranberries, sour cherries, apricots along with raisins and prunes. I not only love these as food but since my prolonged stay in hospital a few years ago, from which I emerged with that well-known pain in the nether region that begins with a 'p' or an 'h', depending on how posh you want to be, regular eating of dried fruit has been (doctors, please note) a total and perfect remedy.

Now I happen to live near to the world's greatest purveyor of dried fruit, W. Martyn's of Muswell Hill, in North London. Mr Martyn purveys a lot of other glorious comestibles but let's stick with dried fruit for the moment. And raisins. Mr Martyn is not content to flog any old raisin. Mr Martyn makes extensive enquiries round the raisin and sultana wholesalers of London so that he can offer his customers the best.

I have conversations with Mr Martyn about raisins (and the fortunes of Arsenal football club too. It's another way for me to have a good day, done by joining the dots between my love for football and my love for dried fruit). Mr Martyn is the only person I've ever met who has discovered giant yellow sultanas. He tells me that they come from Chile. Apparently, this means that the supply cannot be guaranteed. Mr Martyn tells me that sometimes giant yellow Chilean sultanas get lost on the high seas, or locked in warehouses in Tilbury. When this happens, these are times for grieving – which for some reason may well coincide with Arsenal losing.

But then, the sun rises, the tempests abate, the bonded Tilbury warehouse is unlocked and Mr Martyn gets in his supply of giant yellow Chilean sultanas. And so it is that when I open Michael's dried fruit cupboard, there they are, each sultana with a smile on its face, saying, 'Eat me.' And, I have plans. I am going to drop and scatter a few giant yellow Chilean sultanas onto my four scoops of Belgian chocolate ice cream. It's an experiment. I want to know if this is a great combination. It's high risk, though. I could ruin both. The ice cream could be upstaged by the sultanas. The sultanas could be smothered by ice cream. High risk indeed.

But I press on regardless. I'm not a gambling man, but I'm thinking that the odds are good. I scatter the sultanas. I dig in. The spoonful of ice cream has something like three giant yellow Chilean sultanas mingled with the shards of chocolate. Then it's into the mouth.

There's a moment when I pause to take it in. Has it worked? Or have I ruined the day?

It has worked. The flavours match perfectly. These sultanas – I have omitted this from the story so far – are sweet and sour. They are fruity-lemony, with an acid edge. So the full meld here is chocolate, sultana and lemon. But then, as with all good experiments, there's an unexpected outcome. I was all prepared for an interesting clash of texture: the freezing-melting of the ice cream with the chewiness of the sultana. But something else happened. The ice cream has frozen the sultanas. They have turned into resistant, toffee-like pebbles. So as the chocolate melts, the sultana in this frozen state persists, and can only give up its flavour if I give it a good old chew. What's happened is that the whole business of this ten o'clock snack has slowed down. It's become impossible to consume Belgian chocolate ice cream laced with giant yellow Chilean sultanas quickly. It can't be rushed. It has to be taken step by step. With pauses. While the flavours and textures blend.

I'll leave you with that image, if I may.

I was going to say that experiments have given us civilisation as we know it: the discovery of electricity with Signor Alessandro Volta (see P is for Play), the discovery of the DNA double helix with Franklin, Crick and Watson, the discovery of penicillin, the Covid vaccine, the wheel, the umbrella ... but there isn't time or space (which, I discover, thanks to experiments, could well be the same thing. Time and space, that is. They could be the same thing. I did just say that).

SUGGESTIONS

Here are some experiments for you to try:

– Stand upright, with your legs apart. Make sure your shoulders are relaxed and 'down'. See if you can lose tension from around your neck and shoulders. Breathe in through your nose and out through your mouth. Put some resistance into breathing out by pursing your lips as if you're playing a trumpet. This is called 'trilling'. Try singing as you trill. Now very, very slowly raise your arms up from by your sides to horizontal. And then lower them very, very slowly. Ask yourself, can you feel anything change anywhere between your sternum and your pubic bone? Or in your buttocks? Or down the back of your legs? Is this pleasant? Unpleasant? Experiment with other arm movements, or by doing the same lying down. Experiment with breathing in and out even more deeply. Experiment doing it quickly.

– What's the best way to cook rice the way you like it? Following the exact instructions on the packet? Using methods in cookbooks or online? Combining several different methods?

- Doing it the way your grandmother does it? What can you do the next day with cold rice?

- Microwave it? Mix it with chopped vegetables (cooked? Not cooked? Both?)? Add balsamic vinegar? Vinaigrette? Mayonnaise? Mustard? Chutney? Curry sauce? Hummus? And have you experimented with different kinds of rice? Some people have never tried arborio rice! How is this possible?!

- At the next meeting you go to, experiment with behaving in a way that you've never behaved before. Not in a horrible way. What happens if you, for example (an example relevant to me!), say much less, listen more, only speak if you have something constructive to say? If you're someone who hardly ever says something in meetings, what will happen at the next meeting if you make a point of saying what you really think?

F

is for Fiction

This is the scene: I am about to read a story to my three-year-old son. I don't know what story this is going to be because he chooses. He has a pile of books to choose from, some on his shelves and some, indeed, in a pile. That's because he not only chooses books for us to read to him, but he sometimes sits on the floor browsing through books to read to himself. This is a moment I have been looking forward to. A moment when 'the day' seems to disappear, and we're in a tunnel, absorbed in a book. But what book? Will it be a book where I will pore over the pictures, wonder about the words, speculate about what the makers of the book are trying to get at? Or will it be that old shoe catalogue I gave him which has page after page of shoes for the larger man? (I'm size 12 and a half UK.)

This is the moment when my son knows that it's reading-to-him time. He goes over to the pile and picks out the book that he's been choosing night after night. It's *Where the Wild Things Are*. In case you don't know it, it's a book by Maurice Sendak, about a boy who at the beginning of the story is naughty – he's dressed in a 'wolf-suit' and says that he wants to eat his mother up. Max's mother calls Max a 'wild thing' and sends him to bed without eating anything. In his room, a forest starts to grow. He gets on a boat and sails away to the land where the wild things are, who say that they want to eat Max up, but he tames them and they all have a 'wild rumpus' together. After this 'rumpus', Max feels lonely and wants to be where 'someone loved him best of all'. So he sails back home to his room where he finds that there's some supper waiting for him and it's still hot.

I could well have read Emile this book at least 20 times but I resist trying to tease him away from it. There must be a reason why he keeps choosing the book. No matter how much I enjoy this ritual, if I'm honest with myself, I must get the point: this moment is for him. But why was it that each time I had read it to him on all those previous occasions, he was quiet? Part of me thinks that I'm not only at bedtime reading-time but at detective-time. What makes him click? I go over the 'facts': he hadn't said anything. He hadn't joined in; he hadn't asked questions. He had looked very closely at the pictures and listened to me reading the story. In a situation like that, whether you're a parent, grandparent, caring adult, sibling, you have no real idea what the young child is thinking.

I think about this moment, as the birth of the way all of us get to understand what a story is. When I say, 'this moment', I don't mean that this moment will be identical for all of us. Far from it, this moment may be in front of the TV, looking at a story being told on a video on a phone, hearing parents and grandparents tell each other stories about their lives; it may be at a puppet show, or at playgroup singing a song that tells a story – or any other number of different places. In each of these situations, with a very young child, it may really be almost impossible to know what's going on in their minds, though every now and then we get a glimpse that appears to shed light on it. In so doing, it sheds a light on what we all make of stories, whether as child or adult. And this can be the makings of a good day, whether that be for the child or you, or both.

So I'm reading *Where the Wild Things Are* again and, I'll admit, I was expecting the same silent response. As I'm reading, I am thinking, *I wonder why Emile wants this story again and again?* Is it because he's puzzled? Or is he bothered by something? Does he think that if he hears and sees the book again, he'll solve a problem that he has with it? Is he horrified by the 'wild things' and wants to look at them just to test himself whether he can cope with looking at them? Or what? Shall I ask him? No, he's busy figuring something out.

Then, on this, let's say, twenty-first occasion of hearing the words and looking at the pictures, we get to that moment when Max feels lonely and 'wanted to be where someone loved him best of all'. And he calls out – remember, it's the first time he's said anything – 'Mummy!'

Wow! I'm bowled over. A flood of thoughts streams through my mind. Why did he say 'Mummy!'?

In one sense, this is entirely obvious and nothing to remark on. Little Max is miles away from home, he's in the company of four monsters who said they wanted to eat him up. The best thing to do if you're lonely (or scared) is head home to the person who loves you, and that's 'Mummy!' All obvious.

But there are intriguing problems with saying it's obvious. I remember that I'm in detective mode.

First of all, in the book, we never see a 'mummy'. She is, as it were, offstage, out of view, not in any of the pictures. We know that a 'mother' exists because Max said that he wanted to eat her up, and we know that she has responded by sending him to bed without anything to eat. Tough love, Max! Do we know anything else about this 'mother'? Not really. It's true that a 'supper' appears at the end of the book, but it doesn't say for certain that the 'mother' cooked it, and there is, as I say, no picture of her.

This is very intriguing.

I go on: for Emile to have said, 'Mummy!' means that Emile has inferred that Max was thinking of *his* mother when the narrative says he 'wanted to be where someone loved him best of all'. At some level or another, my three-year-old Emile has figured that Max's mother loves him best of all. But the story doesn't say that, and there are no pictures 'saying' that, which it could have done, say, by showing us some kind of physical show of love, a hug or cuddle or some such.

Even more intriguing.

There is also the matter of the fact that the book says 'mother' and Emile has said 'Mummy'. Emile calls his mother 'Mummy'. So has Emile fused Max's mother with his mother? When he looked at the picture of Max looking glum and heard me say that line, did Emile, in a sense, become Max, so that in his mind, he (Emile) was lonely and thought, 'What would I do if I was Max? I would be lonely too. And if I want to be with "someone who loved" me "best of all", who would that be? My mummy.'

So the answer to that question, 'who would that be?' is not '*his* mother' but, intriguingly, '*my* [implied] mummy'.

Interestingly, also, is the fact that the book doesn't pose that as a question. The full sentence runs: 'And Max the king of all wild things was lonely and wanted to be where someone loved him best of all.'

No question there.

So if there is no question, why has Emile come up with something that sounds like an answer? What there is, instead, is a very significant word: 'someone'. It's significant because it's vague, and because it's vague it has the quality of beckoning to us, inviting us to think: who might that 'someone' be? This is what authors and scriptwriters call 'reveal–conceal'. It's one of the most important motors in all storytelling: at the very moment the book or film etc. 'reveals' something, it might also conceal. Here, in that sentence, the words have revealed that Max yearns to be 'where' he'll be loved 'best of all', but they conceal who he might be thinking of.

What's happened on this particular reading with Emile is that he's filled in the gap. That involves inferring, figuring, deducing, interpreting. Hurrah for that! This book has got his mind racing. I'm a dad. I love the idea of my three-year-old's mind racing. This is turning into a very good day.

I think on: Emile could have filled that gap with some other people from his life: the cat, his sister – dare I say, his dad?

Or anyone else. I'm going to guess, as you probably would, that there are two main reasons why he's said 'Mummy!' One is that the only other person in Max's life in the book is his mother and second that Emile's 'prime carer' has been his mummy. Thus the fusion.

My mind harks back to those other readings of the book, when Emile said nothing. I posed the possibility that he was trying to figure out something. This is purely guesswork on my part, and anyway, he could have been trying to figure out many things. If you spend any time poring over it, the book is puzzling in many ways. I'm puzzled by it. That's why I don't mind reading it over and over again. Why or how does a forest grow in his room? Who or what are the wild things? How come they don't eat Max up? If you've never been sent to bed without having anything to eat (as Emile never had been), you might wonder why Max's mother does that. And why is Max's bedroom so bare? You might wonder how you would behave if you met some wild things in a forest. Would you know how to tame them in the way that Max does? Going back to the moment when Max says that he wants to eat his mother up, you might wonder if you've ever wanted to eat your mother up? And then the end of the book: you might wonder, where is the mother (or 'Mummy')? Yes, Max has been naughty, but he's been on a huge adventure, dealt with some very dangerous monsters and here you are back home. Might not Mummy/mother be glad to see you? Hot supper is nice but … but … is it the real deal? I mean, is it the proof that 'someone loved you best of all'? Perhaps, perhaps not. This might worry me. I may only have the question and not an answer.

Indeed, there may well be no definitive answer to that question and, because it's a story, there doesn't have to be. (I'll say in passing that one of the great illusions of 'criticism' of the kind that we often had to do at school, is that there must be or should be a definitive answer to every question about a story!)

So who knows what had been going through Emile's mind on all those other occasions! Maybe it's my illusion that it was one or any of these questions I've posed. Whatever was going on, there was clearly some kind of resolution for him in revealing (discovering?) that what Max wanted was his mummy. That moment when Emile said that, he was going through some kind of thought process that meant: 'If I was Max and I was in that situation with those wild things, then I would want to be where someone loved me best of all and that "someone" would be my mummy.'

We have a word for this – 'identification'. We often say, when we're watching a film or reading a novel, that we 'identified' with a character or we identified with a certain moment when that character faced a problem, a difficulty or a great success, or when that character was in some kind of dilemma and couldn't make up their mind. We say, 'I identified with her' or 'I identified with that moment' or some such.

Is this one of the great satisfactions of fiction? Emile clearly thought so. He was, I reckoned, having a good day, and returning to our favourite novels, or finding new ones to explore, can be part of a good day for all of us. Fiction can give us an opportunity to feel that identification.

What else can we learn from that moment? We love 'reveal–conceal' because it plays to our intelligence (in the broadest sense of the word). That is, to our awarenesses: an awareness of what's going on in the story; an awareness of how things in the story relate to things in our own lives; an awareness that though things 'relate' from story to life and back again, there are differences: a story isn't life and life isn't a story; an awareness that a story is an experience and an experience is something we can learn from; an awareness that though a story might be full of danger for the character(s), you, as the reader, watcher or listener, survive; an awareness that though you go off and do loads of different things, some stories – like books and films – stay the same, meaning that you can check and recheck whether you 'got it right' or whether the feelings you had the first time are the same as the next time or the time after that.

In fact, one thing we often do in the face of story (it's possible our human minds find it impossible not to do this), is that we predict what might happen in the narrative, as we go along. Thinking of Emile and *Where the Wild Things Are*, and his first reading/hearing/looking at the story: it's very unlikely that he would have been able to predict what was going to happen next. The book, for a first, very young, reader, is full of surprises: being sent to your room, getting in a boat, meeting wild things, realising that they want to eat you up, taming them, getting away ... and so on. All surprises. But what happens to the surprises each subsequent time you read or hear the book? They become less surprising; you can predict what's coming next. You have the satisfaction of having 'got' this thing. It's become that story you've figured out – possibly, in a sense, you've 'overcome' the story.

What you will have done here is what we all do when we encounter stories after we're about two years old: we make comparisons between them. We start to figure that one story is 'like' another. This takes us through childhood, teen years and into adulthood. When I read *Where the Wild Things Are*, 'shadows' lurk in and around and behind the book. A hero who 'transgresses' at the beginning, sails off on a journey, encounters some monsters, overcomes them and comes home? And comes home to a place which may not be entirely how he might have wanted it? The shadow there for me is *The Odyssey*. This may or may not have been in Sendak's mind. For the moment, this is my thought.

There may also be 'shadows' in specific moments or scenes: little guy meets big guys? – thousands of stories from 'David and Goliath' to Hollywood blockbusters like *The Bourne Identity* where the 'little guy' battles against an 'organisation'. A yearning to be loved by someone 'best of all'? Millions of stories! And so on.

This means that one of the delights of stories and fiction is that we keep making comparisons. There are comparisons across from story to story and across from story to life. I could see that clearly when Emile said 'Mummy' of course, but if we look even more closely, we can see that in order for him to be able to do that, he had to 'select' something from the book and select something from his life and find common ground between the two people (Max and himself) or the two situations. The emotion being expressed is the yearning to be loved by someone. In some way or another, Emile had to select that emotion from what he could hear me reading to him and link it to that feeling he had when thinking about his 'mummy'. So, it's not only person to person, the 'someone' in the book to his 'mummy'. Really it has to be the feeling being expressed that is the common ground between the two things. I'm going to make a huge claim about this: I'm going to suggest that this is one of the ways in which we acquire wisdom. We make comparisons between moments, we select a feeling or an idea from one story and discover why or how it's in common with another story, or how it's in common with a moment in your life. The moment we do that, we're on the road to making generalisations about life. Instead of thinking that there is something unique and alone about Max or about me (Emile), I spot things in common, shared by both of us. Sendak dropped an abstract word into the story – 'love'. Well, it's a word that can feel quite concrete with 'acts of love' or it can feel quite abstract if we say things like 'I want to be loved best of all' by someone!

So what I'm saying here is that a story can often take us towards abstract thought through the feelings we have as we read. Of course, another route to abstract thought can come through reading about … abstract thought! Philosophy and the like. Stories might well offer a route to some abstract ideas a different way: through the feeling and sensation of a moment in one story and a moment in another story, or from a story to a moment in our lives – just as Emile showed.

I know I had a good day that day. I'm pretty sure (I can't be 100 per cent certain) that Emile had a good day too.

SUGGESTIONS

The first one (and I'm bound to say this, aren't I?) is to read a book you read (or was read to you) when you were a child. If you haven't done this, it can be an emotional moment – shocking, even. You might find yourself not just entering the world of that book, but you enter into the kind of child you were. You remember the emotions you had, because you were that kind of child. If your thoughts and feelings are different now, as an adult, you can compare your 'then' with your 'now'. It's *Emil and the Detectives* for me!

But of course it's great to reread and rediscover any of books we've read before from any part of our lives. One of the features of living in the 'cult of the new' is that we can sometimes imbibe a sense that old stuff is boring or is 'no longer relevant'. Go for it. Reread the book that you once read. (I'm very happy rereading *King Lear.*)

Related to this: the book that we didn't finish. Was it because you thought it was rubbish, too hard, you weren't in the right mood, or you were too busy? How about giving it one more go? If it's a book from a previous era, perhaps now you have a better sense of what that era was like (e.g. the 1930s) so the book may feel very different now. (I still haven't finished Dante's *Divine Comedy*. It's on my list of 'to finish reading'.)

G

is for Grounded

One day, I woke up and found myself trying to remember when I first heard someone somewhere describe someone's character as 'grounded'. When did it become a thing that people said about other people? And what did it mean, anyway?

It seemed to me that in my lifetime, it suddenly became a new way to say that someone was sensible but, more than that, it also gave the impression that this person knew who they were, and couldn't be blown off course. And did it also have the hint of that other meaning when we say that someone is well grounded 'in' something, like physics or Latin, where it means being knowledgeable about a subject?

I wasn't looking for a technical definition or explanation for 'grounded' but more what I might call a 'usage meaning' – that's to say, how people first started using the word and what they meant by it. In the end, I went to the *Oxford English Dictionary*, which is wonderful for telling us about when people first started using a word in writing, but, as its editors admit, it can't keep up with the new things that we say to each other – the oral examples.

This is what the *OED* gives as its first usage for this particular definition of the word:

1976: 'Trungpa's position is that "psychedelics" are too trippy, whereas people need to be *grounded*; everything is uncertain enough as it is.' A. Ginsberg in *New Age Journal*, April 25/3

And that A. Ginsberg is none other than the beat poet Allen Ginsberg.

The *OED* gives as its definition of this meaning, 'grounded: of a person, having his or her feet on the ground'. Was it Ginsberg who took the idiom 'he's got his feet on the ground' and turned it into 'grounded'? We'll never know.

But then I got to thinking about how you get to feel grounded, or get to be a grounded person, because it's quite a desirable thing to be. In fact, if you're grounded, it's one of the ways you can have a good day. So first, how do you ground yourself? I mean, we know only too easily how we might 'get blown off course', 'lose our way', get swayed by what other people are saying. It might be because we drink too much or take drugs, or it might be because something in our upbringing made us inclined that way. If a forceful person comes into our lives, we can be easily convinced by them. We might even end up saying to ourselves things like, 'I don't know who I am.' Back with that Sheryl Crow song I mentioned in B is for Bad Days, when she was wondering if the things she had seen were ever real.

That could be a definition of not being grounded and not having a good day. If we want to, we can take it from that song that going on the road with a 'vending machine repair man' and 'living on coffee and nicotine' is one way to 'blow you off course' ... unless you're a 'grounded' person.

I'm very used to enjoying stories (memoirs and films in particular) of people being on the road, wandering about, exploring, getting lost. It is one way to have good days. I've done a bit of it myself (see J is for Journeys) but here with this word 'grounded', there's a sense that if you go wandering (literally or metaphorically) and you're not 'grounded', you might get yourself into some kind of trouble. People might use you. You might lose a sense of who you really are.

Again, think of Sheryl Crow when she was feeling like a stranger to herself.

That doesn't sound too good. I'd call that 'unsafe'.

So can we engineer how to become grounded or less ungrounded? Are there some good days to be had by doing this?

Let's try some things. I tell myself that I am not strange in being someone who can close their eyes and think myself back into the home I lived in from the age of about 18 months until I was 16. That is, from 1948 until 1962. It's not just that I can see bits and pieces of the flat we lived in but I can also feel and smell tiny details of it. If I concentrate, I can sense that I am there. One example: when I was about eight or nine, my parents bought a new carpet for the living room. It seemed very luxurious and special. I remember my parents talking about the 'pile' of the carpet. I used to like sitting on it, digging my fingers into it, down past the vertical fibres to get to the backing. As I say that, I can feel the sensation on my fingertips and nails. I can see the colour of the carpet, a rusty red.

It's just a carpet. But then it's not just a carpet. It's the carpet that I sat on or walked over hundreds of times, on my own, with my brother, with my parents, with my grandparents, with my parents' friends, with my friends. Even though the carpet is just a bunch of fibres sewn together, it's intermingled with all these faces and voices, words and thoughts.

And something else: my parents were what we would now call 'upwardly socially mobile'(!). When they were young, I doubt very much they ever had a carpet like this. Rugs, maybe, but not a 'pile' carpet. But even that doesn't give the picture. My parents not only became materially better off. They crossed a style barrier. For reasons I haven't ever fully understood, they became 'arty'. They became fascinated by and immersed in art, music, poetry, architecture, film, song, pottery, theatre – and this is where the carpet comes in, in 'good taste'.

Looking back on it, I can sense how they started talking more and more of things having to look right. They worked with potters and bought pottery. They put reproductions of paintings on the walls. They spent many hours choosing wallpaper, chairs and … the carpet. If you lived in London in the 1950s and you had become this type of person, there was one place in particular where you went: Heal's. It was a cathedral to 'good taste'. I went with my parents when they chose chairs, a sofa, curtains and … the carpet. I wondered how they had become so knowledgeable about 'pile' and 'fabric', and 'draw cords' and 'underlay'. And why did it matter anyway?

When finally their good-taste haul came home from Heal's and was fixed and laid and placed, people came over and commented on it all. They stroked and prodded the 'chair covering'; they fanned the curtains out. When my friends came over, though, they stared at it all. It looked weird. It didn't look like their homes and they said so.

Why am I going on about this? Because, whether I'm comfortable with it or not, this is about identity. My friends understood that, even if I didn't. So when it comes to thinking about 'knowing who I am', then being able to 'find' that carpet in my mind, and what it goes with in terms of my parents, it's a bit of firm 'ground'. I stand on the carpet.

There's more! I can walk myself round the flat.

Home.

The hard black phone. I can remember the telephone number: Pinner 1826.

I can run my hand over the 'distemper' on the lavatory wall, and it was on my bedroom wall too. I can lick my finger and wipe the distemper with my fingertip. Then, when my parents get 'good taste', I get Paris wallpaper – Eiffel Towers and gendarmes. I can hear the 'geyser' spluttering hot water into the bath, limescale on the tip of the spout. I can smell our cat dying on my bed – my bed with its red 'hospital' blanket, that in winter became bedewed with condensation from my breath.

I see the man peeing on the moon on an inn-sign, in Bruegel's painting *Netherlandish Proverbs* on our front room wall.

I hear my father saying to me, 'Why do we live here?' And I say, 'I don't know. I'm seven. Why would I know?'

We seem to live mostly in two rooms, separated by a corridor that my brother and I use for racing Dinky cars. My brother knows all their names: Lanchester, Buick, Austin …

One end of this corridor is the kitchen where we eat and where wet clothes hang on the 'airer', which is hoisted to the ceiling and tied off on a hook by the door. It's near enough to the cooker so that I go to school in shirts that smell of liver and onions. At the other end of the corridor is the 'front room' where the rust red carpet now sits. My father is annoyed by what he calls the 'phoney bloody Tudor windows'. 'Hah!' he says. 'Hundreds of diamond-shaped panes. Every one of them lets in a draught!'

To defeat the bloody windows, my father spends months fitting a 'Courtier' stove which has a beautiful black enamel front and two doors, each with mica windows. It's my job to empty the ash pan. All other stove work is taken on by my father, who kneels at the Courtier as if it's a domestic shrine, polishing it and patting it, and repeating, 'Not a bad old fire there, lad,' which we shorten to N.A.B.O.F.T.L.

My parents have a good-taste Heal's armchair each. My mother sits on one, knitting us jumpers and socks. My father sits on the other, reading, making notes and smoking. As the ash falls onto his front or down the side of the chair, my mother says, 'Look at your father surrounded by his droppings. He won't do anything about it till he's treading in it. Once he gets that tukhes of his stuck in the chair, he can never get it out again' ['tukhes' = bum in Yiddish].

In winter, we heat the kitchen with a coke fire that's lit by a metal tube with holes in it, which fires blue flames at the coke till it glows red. The window looks out over a backyard with a coal bunker, which I climb into and go to the moon, repeating my brother's and my favourite lines from the Light Programme's *Journey into Space*. 'Lemmy? Lemmy? Are you there, Lemmy?'

Beyond the yard is a back alley surfaced with brown pebbles where I play ball games with the butcher's son, Keith; the United Dairies horse that pulls the milk-cart stamps and snorts; and it's where my brother dubs the owner of the off-license Mr 'Accelerating-past-the-dustbins', on account of his wild speeding into our cul-de-sac.

Next door to him are the couple who tip-toe over the pebbles like it's a dung heap, him in his suede shoes, her in her black high heels. Mum looks at the photo on the front of her latest knitting pattern: 'Oh look, it's him. Suede-shoes!' And it is. In a Fair Isle sleeveless jumper that Mum is knitting for me.

'Are you sure it's not Dirk Bogarde?'

'No, that's him, all right.'

Underneath the kitchen window is the 'flap', a home-made surface that folds up and out, where I stand and help my mother make fruit cake, pickles and jam. In the corner is the larder which my mother says keeps the milk fresh. It doesn't. The milk goes sour. If I try to throw it away, she dives in and grabs it off me, pours it out into a bowl and sips what I think is white sick, sighing, saying, 'Ooh, it reminds me of my mother's smetana' – which I now know was the sour cream from a faraway place my father calls the 'heim' – Poland, Lithuania, Russia …

One year my parents buy what I thought then and still think is one of the first 'Formica' tables ever to reach the UK. I've got it in my office.

Food can end up in prickly moments. My father looks into the distance and says, 'Ah! My bubbe's cholent.' Bubbe is granny. Cholent is a lamb and barley dish – not that I knew that then, because my father saying this prompts my mother to say, 'Cholent? Your bubbe's cholent? Don't think I'm going to stand by the cooker for 24 hours cooking you cholent. Your bubbe spoiled you. Remember this, I'm not your bubbe.'

At this, my father turns to us and says in indignation, 'What did I say? What did I say wrong? All I said, was "my bubbe's cholent". What's wrong with saying that?'

Did he ever find out?

He also said that the estate agents who owned the shop downstairs were called 'Norman and Butt'. True. My father explained that Norman was the one with all the ideas, and the thing is, he said, his partner kept coming up with reasons as to why the ideas were no good, 'Bu-u-u-t,' he would say.

Downstairs, there's a door that leads through from the hallway by our back door. If I look through the door, I can see Norman and Butt at work. But I don't know which is which. Which one has all the ideas? And which one says, 'Bu-u-u-t'?

I can't be sure that remembering all these details – and thousands more – makes me 'grounded' or not. I have a strong sense that it does. I know that whatever happens to me, I've still got the details and I've gone through my life knowing that they're there. I also have a sense that they can't be taken away from me, unless I get dementia or Alzheimer's of some kind. I know that too.

I also know that I love thinking, talking and writing about this stuff, this good day stuff.

SUGGESTIONS

I've already talked about breathing but you can extend and adapt it here too. Most of the day, we don't notice we're breathing. Quite right too. If we spent all day thinking about breathing, we wouldn't do anything else. The thing is how to get yourself into 'now' and attached to where you are. Depending on what senses you've got (and I'm very aware in my post-Covid life that I've lost a lot of sight and hearing), one activity to get into is being 'out there', in the world, in a park, up a hill, by the sea, in a garden, and whether you're walking, sitting or standing, just start off concentrating on your breathing. Imagine that it's your breathing that is giving you the right to be there! This is you and your presence.

Play with your breathing. Try different ways. See if some kinds of breathing make you feel more 'in the world' than others. See what kind of breathing is more enjoyable than others.

If you stretch, or lift things (rocks, tins of baked beans, chairs), breathe out when you lift. As you fill the space that you make, does that make you feel more 'here'?

Talking of filling the space, another way to feel 'here' and grounded is through thinking you're in a box. If you're in a huge box, stretch to the very edge of the box – arms, hands, legs, back – fill the box. Now make the box very small. You squeeze into it. Then it's so small, all you can do is fit your fingers into it. Stretch them to the very edge.

Do you know how I do this last 'in the box' thing? It's every time I perform *We're Going on a Bear Hunt*, usually in front of at least 400 children. If you know the words, you can use them to help you do this 'filling the space' thing. At the end of it, you are in the world, and, yes, grounded!

H

is for Hummus

I'm going to imagine I'm in a swimming pool. One end of the pool is labelled 'The Ideal End', the other end is called 'The Good-Enough End'. As I swim about in the pool, I have to decide whether to head for 'The Ideal End' and become an ideal person or go for 'The Good-Enough End' and be a good-enough person.

In fact, in this scenario, there's something else: I can't get out of the pool. I'm stuck in it, endlessly having to choose which end to swim towards. I worry that if I swim towards 'Good Enough', I'll never get to be 'The Ideal'. If I swim towards 'The Ideal End', will I end up thinking that I'll never be 'Good Enough'? Then I start wondering if I'll ever reach 'The Ideal' – it does seem a long way off. And I even wonder if I'll ever reach 'The Good-Enough End' because it feels as if I'm too fed up with myself for not getting to 'The Ideal End' to ever be 'Good Enough'. This feels like a knot. A dissatisfaction knot.

Perhaps you recognise some of this.

But what's this got to do with hummus? Because the dissatisfaction knot doesn't just have to be about yourself. It can be about things, things I want, buy or have. This is a knot that I should try to get out of. Let hummus be my absurd example.

I'll explain. I love hummus. In fact, I can't get through a day without having hummus. Hummus has become a staple food for me. Just as people think of bread or rice as a staple, I think of hummus. In fact, when I was in hospital a few years ago, I couldn't have hummus. It wasn't because I had become allergic to it, and it wasn't because the nurses or doctors banned me. It was because I was in hospital during lockdown, and no one could come into the hospital and give me hummus. Then, because I had been in an induced coma, doctors asked me if I was hallucinating or experiencing delirium. Mostly all I had were some funny and slightly sad dreams, but nothing traumatic. But when I was awake I suffered from Lack-of-hummus Trauma, Hummus Deprivation Syndrome. I tried to tell the doctors about it but they weren't interested.

In the end, I started fantasising about hummus. I conjured up bowls and side dishes of hummus with drizzled olive oil on top, hummus with a slight peppering of paprika on top, hummus spread on flat bread, hummus on the end of a stick of celery … on and on and on. As I lay in my bed, I was also thinking about children's books that I could write when I got out, and for some reason I started to think about a cat who longed for pasta. I gave the book a name: *Rigatoni the Pasta Cat*. A plotline started to form in my mind: Rigatoni is looked after by two women. They know that Rigatoni loves pasta. They feed him pasta. But one day, they have to go away. They arrange for a boy to come and look after Rigatoni, but they forget to tell the boy that Rigatoni loves pasta. The boy just feeds them cat food – which I called 'Good Mews'. (Sorry about that.)

But no pasta.

And Rigatoni starts to get desperate. How can he find someone to give him pasta?

Well, that's the 'problem' of the story, and I 'wrote' the book in my head while I lay in bed in the hospital. Then I came out of hospital, I wrote the story on my computer and it was published.

You may well have realised by now that there is a resemblance between what's going on in the story of Rigatoni the Pasta Cat, and my state of mind thinking about hummus. The funny thing is I didn't realise this until the book came out and I read it through. 'Ah! That's me in hospital wanting hummus,' I said to people.

So, you've got the picture: I love hummus. And I love it so much that I even write stories about loving it, even if the story seems to be about something else.

But I'm stuck in the pool, remember. I'm stuck in the pool of forever hovering between the Ideal and the Good Enough. And this can be about a view of myself, or about things. Now let's apply this to hummus. I'm hovering between longing for the perfect ('ideal') hummus and accepting that this dish of hummus I'm eating right now is good enough. But then, I'll ask myself another question: is it possible to do both? That is, to search for the ideal AND accept that what I have is good enough? (This statement deserves a drum roll in appreciation of such a realisation.)

I think so.

And further, is it possible to strive to be better at something (with some kind of actual or implied ideal in mind) and yet still think you're good enough, if you don't achieve it? I've a feeling that the answer to this question has a lot to do with whether we can ever have a good day.

But let me hold off answering that question by raising another one. Why might we ever think that we are people who strive for something that we know is unattainable, while at the same time always thinking that we aren't good enough? That's absurd, surely. And what if that can apply to things too: why might we strive to have things that we think are perfect and then, when we find that they're not, we can't accept that they're good enough?

In fact, I could claim that, in its own way, this is one of modernity's burdens. We are lumbered with this at almost every turn: as we go about life, aiming to achieve this or that, as we do up our homes, as we go on holiday, as we buy a pair of shoes or indeed a tub of hummus! We might say to ourselves, 'I'm never going to be perfect; I'm always not good enough. This hummus isn't perfect; it's not good enough.' And this all blurs into one. If I'm someone who often laments being not perfect, I may well also be someone who laments the fact I can't find the perfect hummus.

Logically speaking, we probably know what's going on: we are constantly being presented in life and in the media with high-end achievements and claims about perfect places and things that we can buy (whether they are or not!). Some people have called this 'manufacturing desire'. Many things are graded for us with stars: movies, music, services, books (!), holiday homes, pubs, restaurants … Even world-famous film stars, praised for their beauty, envied by millions, yet, when it comes to their acceptance speech for a top award, they reveal that they too can be afflicted by not-good-enough syndrome. On the podium accepting a Golden Globe in 2025, US film star Demi Moore talked of moments when she thought she was 'done' with the acting profession; she had thought she'd achieved all that she could ever achieve. Then she said this: 'In those moments when we don't think we're smart enough or pretty enough, or skinny enough or successful enough, or basically just not enough, I had a woman say to me, "Just know, you will never be enough. But you can know the value of your worth if you just put down the measuring stick."'

So is the problem the 'measuring stick' – constantly measuring our worth (and measuring it against others, I would add), so we can't accept who we are, or that the hummus is good enough?

Earlier in her speech, Demi Moore described a comment that someone had once made towards her as 'corrosive'. In the flow of her speech, she didn't actually say that the measuring-stick mentality is 'corrosive' too but I think she was implying it.

Is there any escape from this? We often want to 'do our best' and 'have the best', so how can we say to ourselves that what we did or had was good enough? If we find we can say it's good enough, there's a big reward waiting for us. The reward is that we don't go about feeling constantly dissatisfied: bad day stuff.

Let's see if thinking about hummus helps resolve this. I can make hummus. It's relatively easy: soak chickpeas overnight, boil them till they're soft, mash them up, mix up that mush with tahini, garlic, lemon juice and olive oil. Serve with a dash of paprika on the top and a few leaves of flat-leaf parsley. But in what proportions? Aha! That's the point. My ideal and your ideal will be different. I like moderate amounts of tahini. Some people like loads. I like to taste the garlic. Some people don't. Some people like it to be ultra-smooth, I like it to be 'rough' in texture. You know what this means? There is no ideal in some kind of objective, universal way. There's choice and bias and preference.

And another thing – this is humiliating for any vestige of the home cook in me – there are some shop or café hummuses that I think taste better than anything I've ever made. I can't even make the ideal for me!

So I'll tell you where I've got to with this. I have sought and found a new state of equilibrium: if I really can't be bothered to go on and on trying to make a hummus that is as good as the hummus at the deli or that café in the high street, then I should accept that the hummus I buy is good enough. Quite clearly, I'm not cut out to be Gordon Ramsay, or a restaurant critic, or even those who turn up their noses at something when they go out to eat.

Unlike these folk, what I do is try to think globally. (I'm not kidding.) I try to say to myself, 'I'm out, I'm hungry. If this food is fresh and OK, then remember there are millions all over the world with not enough food, so this is good enough.' Or, I say, 'We're out with the family (or a group of friends). This is fun. We're having a good time. Globally in my life, this is good. The hummus is good enough.'

In the back of my mind, I may well have that ideal in my mind: the rough texture, the go-easy-on-the-tahini, the full-on garlic, the paprika, the flat-leaf parsley leaves. But so what? There'll be another time, another place. In fact, Michael, I say to myself, you can turn this hunt for the perfect hummus (or any other bit of perfection) into a game, or as a bit of family theatre: Michael and his hunt for the perfect blackcurrant sorbet, the perfect raisin, the perfect bagel ... and so on. And because it's so daft to think such a thing exists, I can enjoy the quest and enjoy the fact that what I've got when I've got it is good enough.

And this, I find, fits with my view of myself. Again and again, through life, I've strived for something that I could do. I don't think that's a bad thing. Then I achieve that thing – and it can really be a very small thing, like making a really good hummus. Even so, even if I do achieve something, the not-good-enough feeling can always creep back in when I strive for the next thing. In other words, the problem isn't really in the matter of whether I achieve or not. Is the problem in thinking that there is an ideal? The history of stardom is littered with people who, even as they achieved all that there was to achieve and achieved what millions of others have yearned to achieve, still thought that they weren't good enough.

So, every time I have a tub of hummus from the supermarket or the deli, or every time I have a dish of hummus in a café or restaurant, I can hold in my head two things at the same time: there's a hummus that I prefer and there's the hummus I'm having right now. And the hummus I'm having right now is good enough because it's the hummus I'm having right now. Tomorrow I might go in search of that hummus I prefer, and that'll be fun too. In the meantime, I'm eating this hummus and having a good day.

P.S. When I was a child, I read the Puffin Story Book version of the King Arthur stories. I loved all that derring-do stuff, but I was puzzled by Sir Lancelot and Sir Galahad. Lancelot seemed to be such a great guy and Galahad seemed to be so boring. Yet, Lancelot wasn't good enough, while Galahad was perfect. (I didn't know the word then, but he was of course the 'ideal'. Galahad got the Holy Grail; Lancelot didn't.) I puzzled over how you could be a great guy but be not good enough, and yet you could be boring but perfect. I'm not sure I ever solved that one.

SUGGESTION

Play the ideal versus the actual game.

Hunt the ideal apple, the ideal beer, the ideal tomato, the ideal hat, the ideal lamp. Enjoy the actual apple, the actual beer, the actual tomato, the actual hat and the actual lamp.

I

is for If

We talk sometimes about having an 'active mind'. A day when it feels as if we're buzzing with thoughts feels good. But what is an active mind? I'm going to suggest that at the core of it is that tiny word 'if'.

'If' is one of those words that doesn't really have a meaning. Linguists put it into the category of 'grammatical words' along with 'the', 'and', 'to', 'as' and the like. It's curious because we know it has meaning of some sort but it's not like the meanings of, say, 'eat' or 'bottle'. The way we can think about 'if' is to remind ourselves of how we use it. Or, as I might say, '*If* I think about the uses of "if", I can find out more about "if".' That last sentence is the 'if' of logical thought.

'You wouldn't feel so cold, if you put a jumper on.' (Logic.)

'If it takes one person one hour to bake one cake, how many people will it take to bake five cakes in one hour?' (Remember those questions in 'verbal reasoning tests'?)

'If he was in the pub at the time, he couldn't have done it.' (The basis of detective work and whodunnits.)

But this last 'if' – which dictionaries will tell you is part of 'conditional' thinking – can be the stuff of imagination and fantasy. 'If I ruled the world ...' (as the song goes), 'If all the world were paper ...' (nursery rhyme) and even 'If I were you ...', which we know is not going to happen!

We're very easy with putting 'if' into phrases which then give us many more meanings:

- 'If only I had thought about that ...' (regret)

- 'If only I was just a bit taller ...' (wishful thinking)

- 'What if everyone here stood up and we all shout as loud as we can?' (suggestion/question)

- 'She walked into the room as if nothing had happened ...' (comparison)

- 'Even if you've got the right ticket, you'll still need your pass' (one thing or circumstance won't be enough)

- 'Only if you've filled in the form!' (a total and necessary condition)

- 'Maybe if you smartened yourself up ...' (possible condition)

And we can play with 'if', as with the brilliantly compressed retort 'as if!' meaning 'that's not going to happen, is it?'

We can say that something or somebody is a bit 'iffy', meaning dodgy or unreliable. In the case of a decision in sport, it means that the decision was possibly not right, or, in the case of food, it might mean it's 'going off' – iffy means off! We can even turn 'if' into an abstract idea, as when we say, 'We're leaving now, no ifs or buts.' Here the phrase means 'no conditions, no exceptions'.

If (!) you want to go even further with the logical side, you can immerse yourself in paradoxes and fallacies. These have wonderful names like, 'What the Tortoise said to Achilles', 'The Crocodile Dilemma', 'The Ship of Theseus', 'Thomson's Lamp' and many others called this or that 'Paradox'.

You have probably guessed that I think that thinking about 'if' or any part of language is in itself fun and a nice way to spend a day or at least part of a day.

But let me go back to that idea of 'if' being at the heart of what we call an 'active mind'. One enemy of good days is 'stasis'. This is when I feel becalmed, immobilised, paralysed even.

I can't seem to do anything, think anything, want anything – or, at best, very little. It's a mysterious feeling because it doesn't seem to come from anywhere or be caused by anything. It's a 'maybe I'll sit here and do nothing' feeling, a 'I won't do the shopping just now' feeling. Or the washing up. Or the bills. Or empty the bin. Or reply to that email.

In itself, there's nothing wrong with any of this. I can even be positive about it and call it 'down time', 'giving my brain a rest', 'taking the weight off my feet'. The problem arises when I'm fed up because I'm doing nothing and doing nothing is making me fed up. I sometimes think that the reason why I make arrangements to do things 'out there' is because I'm afraid that if I've got nothing to do, I won't do anything! If you get me. I mean that I take on things that other people ask me to do, because it's much easier to do things that other people ask me to do than it is to do things for myself and by myself. People who have a 9–5 job, 5 days a week for 40 years or more are wired into this. I only worked like that for two years or so, but I can see that 'doing nothing' at the weekend for them is a right, an entitlement and a treat.

For anyone who's retired or for people who are working part-time, freelance, or being any kind of homeworker or home keeper, these doing-nothing moments can be fine but, as I know, they can also drift into a sense of pointlessness. The simplest thing to do is eat. I fill the emptiness with a cake. And another. Brilliant. Then I feel fed up that I've eaten cake but not done anything.

But why am I fed up about it? Ah well, that's a long story! The main reason is because throughout my childhood and through college, there were voices from parents and teachers saying, 'You've got to get on' (see O is for On). The words 'lazy' and 'bad' were interchangeable. If you were lazy, you were a bad person. But then, why did my parents and teachers think that? This is a huge psycho-social-historical-political question! I learned that work is good. If I work hard, I am virtuous, and people have been learning this for hundreds of years. After all, 'idle hands make work for the devil': bad things will happen if I do nothing; I will commit sins.

Doing nothing in itself is one of the seven deadly sins: sloth! Sloth is one of the devil's mates. When the industrial revolution came along, ideas like this were really handy. We can conjure up a picture of Dickensian factory owners standing at the gates of their factories, welcoming in long lines of men, women and children, saying, 'Lovely to see you, come in, come in, idle hands make work for the devil. Sloth is one of the seven deadly sins …'

What this means is that when I'm doing nothing, I think something's going wrong. Even if I say to myself that I've been conned by the weight of all that psycho-social-historical-political stuff to feel sinful, being rational about it doesn't get rid of feeling bad. I'll have another cake. So if I can't reason my way out of it, what can I do? After all, I'm on the hunt for a good day, aren't I?

The answer is 'if'. The 'what if …' and the fantasy 'if' in particular. 'If' is the generator. I'll lay aside all my misgivings about feeling conned by the weight of history (!), and just accept it that doing nothing is making me fed up. Enter 'if'. One thing I do with 'if' is make lists. Yes, I know a list is not the same as doing the things that are on the list. Yes, I have conned myself in the past with that one: 'Hey I've got a list of all the things I have to do, so that means I've done them.' I've got over that mountain. Lists of 'to do' really are still 'to do' and there can even be sub-lists within lists. If it says, 'do emails', there can be a sub-list of the top emails that I need to deal with. If it says, 'do shopping', then obviously it should list what has to be shopped. This brings focus. Focus is all. This is about actual, real stuff. Things. 'If I get the milk – milk, a real thing, an object, stuff – then people in the house will have that real thing, that object, that stuff to drink and have in their tea and coffee.' By going out, getting the milk, bringing it back, putting it in the fridge, it will turn the wheels, oil the machine, keep things going. And 'if' I do that, it's me that has made that possible.

So I can multiply that. It's not just milk, after all. It's all the other thingy things that are needed or wanted. I've even got over something that took some getting over. We have grown-up offspring at home with us. I'll confess that there have been moments when I felt that perhaps one of them could get the milk. This thought has arisen, for example, when the 20-year-old has gone to the fridge and said, 'Dad, we need milk.' The thought did cross my mind at that moment that a fit 20-year-old who can walk and run for miles, who can go out and – as far as I know – rave, could just possibly walk 200 metres to the nearest place that sells milk, buy it and bring it back. After all, he was the one who spotted the need. I might also think, with my parenting hat on, that 'it would do him good' to get the milk for himself. After all, I don't drink milk. (Not a dietary or faddish thing on my part. I just don't like milk.) But I've got over these feelings. Now, I just think to myself: *I need to get out.* I need to do stuff. If I go to the shop, remember that it's milk that I've come for, buy it, and come back with it, there's going to be at least one person who'll think that's nice. And another thing: one day, when the offspring is older, he's going to have to buy his own milk. Hopefully, he's got decades ahead of him. In that time, there'll be hundreds if not thousands of cartons of milk that he'll have to buy. So why shouldn't he be, for the time being, in a non-buying-milk place?

(I can hear my father's voice in my ear, raging on and off for 50 years or more at various young people he saw as 'sponging off' their parents. I always took it as a warning to me: don't sponge off me, lad. And yet – here's the lovely contradiction – he was a right old softy with me!)

So we've covered the 'if' of lists.

Now the 'if' of fantasy. I think we all need fantasies, dreams, hopes, desires. Yes, I realise that these aren't exactly as we like to think of them – which is as if they are personal or private.

There are huge industries working away at creating and sell-ing fantasies, dreams, hopes and desires to us. You could even argue that the whole of everything is now based on this. That's what 'the economy' is: a dream factory. Think back to milk. Milk used to be stuff that you got from a cow, goat, camel, sheep or yak. Now milk is packaged: 'full fat', 'semi-skimmed', 'skimmed', and then there is a vast array of other 'milks' made from oats, almonds, coconut and any old stuff, some with jokey labels saying 'Shake me!' or 'The boring side' (where the ingre-dients are) to make them more desirable. It's hard to remember that I can get through life just drinking water. Oh, but there are 20 different waters I can buy, too! This tells me that I shouldn't really just be drinking water out of the tap. Drinking water out of the tap will stop the world going round.

And of course it's not only that the mundane things like milk and water are part of the dream factory; we are also plied with images of dream bodies, dream holidays, dream cars, dream houses ... I'm watching TV and I'm thinking, *I can't have any of these. I must be worthless.*

What's hard (impossible?) is to disentangle our own dreams from the dreams we are being sold. Anything at all to do with my personal appearance that I might think of as a personal matter, is intertwined with blokes on TV stroking their newly shaven cheeks, or sliding neatly into a beautiful pair of jeans.

Yes, yes, yes, I know all that but I'm sitting here fed up and I want to believe my fantasies are my own. If I say to myself, 'I would like to be Prime Minister' (actually, I don't), 'I want to be George Clooney' (OK, there is a bit of me that does want to be George Clooney) or any other of these things about what I want to be or what I want to do, then the 'if' sentences matter. For example, I often hear people say to me that they would like to write. I have taught at universities for 30 years working with students, many of whom would like to write – though I should say here that's never been my actual job! I've been working with students who either want to become teachers or who are teachers and they're looking at how to encourage children to read and write. But they are often people who want to write themselves and they ask me about it. I also meet people as I go about who say that they want to write too.

What springs into my mind is the 'if'. If you want to be something, what is it you have to do? That sounds obvious but I've found that a lot of people have a fantasy but don't want to do the doing to get there. Like me and wanting to be George Clooney. I'm not saying that I could be George Clooney (there's a surprise), but let's say that I really, really, really wanted to be a film actor. Then there are certain things I would have to do or could do that would at least make it possible that I could do walk-ons. I could get myself on the list of 'extras' that movies need for crowd scenes. I could try to get an agent. I could audition. I could produce a portfolio of pictures of myself and send them round. It'll be a lot of work. I might meet someone who'll tell me that I'll need to work out for two hours a day to get myself into shape. But I don't do any of those things, do I? Instead, I sit and think, *What if I was George Clooney?* I meet a lot of people like that when it comes to writing. That's fine if you're fine with it! I'm fine with not being George Clooney. (Fairly. Not totally.) But if I was eaten up with it, the problem would be that I wasn't applying the 'if' sentence. 'If I want to be x, I'll need to do y.' It's about reality and focus – which is quite a weird thing to be saying about fantasies.

So back with good days, 'if' sentences are crucial.

SUGGESTION

What happens if (!) you make your 'if list'?

J

is for Journeys

Sometimes, it helps to think in metaphors. I don't know why, unless it's a relief to be able to say that the thing that troubles you is something else. It often feels good to find connections.

After my son died, I wrote this:

We're travellers on the road.
Always on the road.
Sometimes joined by strangers
who become friends who join us for a while.
A day maybe. Maybe more.
Then we part.
Maybe they've another road to go on.
Maybe it's us who turn off.
Either way, we don't see them again.

I know people I've walked with for years.
There are the ones
I knew from when I was tiny.
There are the ones
I knew from when they were tiny.
Some join, some leave.
Some head off,
go on ahead looking back over their shoulders.
Sometimes they let me catch up.
There's one who left altogether.
He was with us for as long as he could

and oh he kept us laughing on the way:
his jokes, his faces, his noise,
he took up half the road, you know.

I'm very, very far from being the first person in the world to see life as a journey. This image came to me out of a fusion of two things: long walks with my parents, and then, later, walks – not so long – with my own children. Many of us remember family walks where we start to string out along the roads and paths. One or two are up front, one or two in a middling position and one or two are stragglers. I can see clearly in my mind's eye my father and brother up ahead on a path by some woods somewhere. I'm with my mother, way, way back.

It's not a sad feeling. As the youngest, it just seems to be the way these walks panned out. There's a hint of something else: at that time, I wouldn't have known that my mother had lost a child, who was older than me but younger than my brother. He was a middle child whom we never knew. Though saying that is not quite right as I was born after this child. Who's to say our parents would have had a third child had he lived? Maybe I was the child to make up for the one they had lost? As we walk along the road, me about 8, my brother 12, we don't know about this lost boy, because neither of our parents have ever mentioned him. There have been no photos, no mementoes, no memorial events and no relatives or friends have ever mentioned him.

One way or another, I have a sense now that my mother treated me as the one she had to protect. The gag was that whenever my brother or father was having a go at me, mum would say, 'Leave him alone. He's tired.' After a while, my brother and father would tag those phrases onto what they said to me if they were telling me what to do. So my brother would say in one flowing run of words, 'Will you tidy your side of the bedroom leave him alone he's tired.'

So, though the scene in my head of the walk – my father and brother up ahead, me with my mother – is nice in itself, it's tinged with these feelings.

Then, when I switch to me being out with my children, I can see in my mind a day when I take Joe (my oldest) and my late son Eddie for a long walk in Derbyshire. I know why I'm doing this. I have realised I've got fed up with myself that I haven't passed on to them a love of going for long walks in the country! I come to think that when they took us for these hikes, my parents relived their youth. They were inner city kids in the 1920s and 1930s who hoped for a better world. At the time, part of this urge was going off in gangs and troupes, to camp and hike. They succeeded in passing this on to my brother and me. I spent many holidays in my teens and early twenties hiking with friends in Wales, the French Pyrenees, Dartmoor and so on. I became hike crazy, all shorts and light-weight orange tent.

And yet here was me, a parent, and I had failed. I hadn't done all the coaxing and cajoling that you have to do to get children to hike and so they hadn't caught the bug. I berated myself that, after all, when I was 11 ('for goodness sake!'), hadn't I sat down with my friend Brian Harrison and planned walks in the Chiltern Hills by getting on a train to Princes Risborough, 'walking the escarpment' (note the technical geological language there, learned from my brother) and coming home on the same day? I got to love the slowness of walking, proud of the skills I'd acquired to read an Ordinance Survey map, and I loved those moments when I'd get to the top of a hill and see over the landscape I had walked on and the places I was heading for.

But I hadn't passed on any of that.

Yet, here we were out on the road. My older boy, Joe, is being tolerantly agnostic about it. He has always seemed to be able to view me with a raised eyebrow: as if he's saying to himself, 'It's crazy but it's what Dad does ... just go along with it.' But if Eddie wasn't happy about something, he said so. Straightaway. On this occasion I can hear him saying, 'What's the point of walking? It's really slow. And you get tired. What's the use of that?'

Both very good points. And I didn't have much of an argument – at least not one to convince an eight-year-old. He liked running about and falling over. The moment we'd get into the country, that's what he did: run to and fro very fast, fall over and then roll on the ground. Yippeee! You can't convince someone like that, that plodding slowly up a hill is really interesting. I tried to say something convincing. I said that when you walk, you notice stuff.

'Look,' I said, 'that's a dry stone wall. No mortar. That's amazing.'

'No, Dad, that's not amazing. It's dry.'

Again, a nice memory. It's funny and I can enjoy my failure to pass on this enthusiasm across generations but also, again, it's tinged with sadness. It's an Eddie memory that I can't share with him because he's gone.

Sometimes people talk to me, hinting at wanting to know how it's possible to carry on, to have good days, if you've lost a child. Those of us who have, talk about how the sadness never goes but we each find ways of 'living with it'. In my case, it's as if I find a place to put it so that it doesn't hurt so much. It's like when you have a pain in your leg, but if you move to another position it doesn't hurt so much. A good day can be had.

The poem at the beginning also coincides with one of my favourite books: Chaucer's *Canterbury Tales*, where a group of pilgrims make their way from London to Canterbury telling each other stories. Here the metaphor of life being a journey is in the shadows, and the sense of what life is all about comes from the stories, which, when seen together, give us a view of late medieval life. And do you know something, guess what I used to say to my parents when I was a tired and bored walker, aged about eight? I used to ask them to sing songs or tell stories. Then, thinking about that now, I can see my father saying, 'Once upon a time there were some chickens and a cockerel called Chanticlere ...' I didn't know then that he was telling me one of the stories from *The Canterbury Tales*. Of course he was! We were walking along a road – not on a pilgrimage as such, but 'wending our way', nevertheless. I enjoy connections like that, too.

Another place for connections is when I do my family history research (see M is for Memories). Again and again, I find people who've made once and for all journeys of the big migration journey kind. Very nearly all of us migrate at some time or another in our lives, even if all we do is move next door or across town. As I look at my tree, I see big journeys from Poland to Newcastle, Lithuania to London, Poland to France, London to the USA, London to South Africa, sometimes to stay, sometimes to try it for a while and come back, and, in the case of deportations from France and within Poland, to death in Auschwitz.

One journey is a mystery. My father's uncle and aunt moved from Poland to France. Around the time the Second World War broke out, they migrated, along with millions of others, to western France. In France, to commemorate such a mass journey, it's called 'L'Exode' (Exodus). Once the Nazis had divided up France, life for my great-uncle and aunt became precarious so, as I have discovered from documents in local archives, they went on the run. They left Niort in western France and made their way to Nice in south-east France. According to Google, it's 982 km by the shortest route by road. The paperwork that I have shows that they went missing in July 1942 and they were arrested in Nice in September 1943.

This is a real journey under terrifying conditions but all I can ever know about it is that it happened. For me, it has to be an imaginary journey. So I imagine it.

I don't know whether they managed to get a lift – if so, how? Or were they able to beg for lifts, one after the other? It's also just about imaginable that they walked. If you could walk 20 km a day, that would take you 49 days. If you could only manage 10 km a day, it would take just short of 100 days. So now I picture these two people, newly married, heading across France, through landscapes I know, the beautiful rivers, valleys, mountains I've walked on or near; there are towns I've hitch-hiked through. I 'see' the streets, the houses, the tiled roofs, the shutters, the shop signs and the big painted advertisements for Perrier, Suze and Dubonnet. Perhaps they have to dodge soldiers and guards. Do they have false papers that conceal the fact that they are Jewish? Presumably they've taken off the yellow stars that they had been compelled to wear.

In one of the letters that my father's uncle writes to his brother in America, he says that he's running out of money. So how are they managing to survive? Do they do casual work on the way? As farm workers, perhaps?

I see them sleeping in fields and barns. Are there secret signs used by the Resistance that they get to know, which enable them to hide, stay and move on?

I have no idea. It's like a film. I imagine dialogue. Two people, in love, desperate to survive, urging each other on. They've heard of an imagined place where Jews are going and never come back from. People call it by a nonsense name: 'Pitchipoï'. People say, 'Nous n'irons pas à Pitchipoï!', meaning 'we won't go to Pitchipoï'. They make progress – is it summer? The smell of thyme on the hillsides. Desperately hot. Or winter with snow?

And then, finally, with huge relief, they get to Nice, where they know they will be protected by the Italians who, in spite of demands from Adolf Eichmann, are refusing to round up Jews. They end up in one of the large high hotels that have been taken over by the refugees as there are no tourists. It's all the grandeur without the luxury. I imagine people sleeping on the stairs underneath beautiful chandeliers.

And then, suddenly, it all becomes terrifying again. The Italians have to leave and the Nazi troops and SS guards arrive. My great-uncle and aunt are interrogated, sent on another journey, this time by train to a transit camp, and then from there they're put into cattle trucks and deported on a 'convoy' (Convoy 62) to Auschwitz.

This last I can imagine because survivors have written about this fearful journey over several days, crammed into the trucks, no food, no water, no toilets. This time I imagine them even more desperate, hanging on to each other, disgusted and ashamed of the filth, starving, riven with worry and incomprehension, imagining ways in which they could or might survive in the place where they're going, whatever that is. And then, when they get there, my father's uncle realises that they have arrived at a place built next door to a town he recognises. It's the town he was born in: in Polish, Oświęcim, in German, Auschwitz.

Finding out about this last terrible journey took me to Paris where I discovered that some Jewish men who were in the Resistance escaped from that train. They broke out of the truck and ran. The father of one of the men banged his head and passed out. The rule in the Resistance was: don't go back. So they left him and ran on. When he woke up, he headed off and reached a farm. He explained what had happened and the owners took him in, at great risk to themselves, because if the SS had found him, they would have been killed. They looked after him and when the SS came, they lied and said he wasn't there. Then when it was all clear, the son took him back to Paris where he rejoined the others.

When I heard this story, I was full of admiration but also what I can only describe as vicarious retrospective envy. I identified with my father's uncle and aunt, and wished that they could have escaped.

You may sense here that a lot of all this involves me going into a reverie. Daydreaming about something, wondering, imagining, creating images, linking them into a narrative. Nearly all of us do this – some a lot, some not so much. Some of us enjoy it. Some are irritated that by doing it, we've wasted time. I would say, though, that daydreaming is vital. We imagine ourselves through life, having a vision of what we could do, might do, should do, or indeed what could have been, might have been and should have been. A lot of what I've said about 'curiosity', 'if' and 'experiment' in this book, involves us daydreaming. When children ask me what subject I was good at school, I say, 'Daydreaming.'

Some daydreaming can be remembering – and I've saved some of that for M is for memories. Another kind can be what I've done here with J is for Journey: I've combined the reverie of memories with the vision of what could have been, what might have been. Some of our daydreams are troubling, of course.

One way to make them less so, I find, is to write them down, as I've done here. As I've said before in the book, part of the trick of having good days is finding ways to not have bad days; being happy by not being unhappy.

SUGGESTION

As you might guess, my suggestion here is 'write them down'. Work on your daydreams. Use them, harvest them, play with them, adapt them, change them, make up music to go with them, draw drawings to go with them ...

K

is for Kvell and Kvetch

My parents used Yiddish words. My father would often encourage my mother to kvell. She was quite self-effacing and sometimes did herself down. 'No,' my father would say, 'you should kvell.' He meant she should be proud. He might say, if one of us did well and it made him feel proud, 'I'm kvelling.'

On the other hand, if I was nagging for more cake, Mum would say, 'Michael, don't kvetch!' Or, my father might turn to my mother and say, 'Why's he being such a kvetch?' Kvetch (sometimes spelled kvetsh) means to whinge, or to be a whingey person.

If you fancy knowing about the origins of words, you can dig around and find that 'kvell' has something to do with water welling up out of the ground like a spring at its source, so when you kvell, you swell with pride. 'Kvetch' is to do originally with pushing, so whingeing is a way to put pressure on people. As you can use these words when you're speaking English, we can be like my father and say 'kvelling' – putting the English 'ing' ending on a Yiddish word. This turns it into what some call 'Yinglish'. To be pinpoint accurate, my parents could have spoken Yiddish but instead, sometimes chose to speak Yinglish.

In my book *Rosen's Almanac*, I explored the idea that we all have family and group ways of talking. Sometimes, we don't even notice these words and phrases but then a situation crops up and we find that they express the flavour of who we are. If you're from Scotland or Northern Ireland and you say that you're 'scunnered', then saying you're 'disgusted' or 'sickened' doesn't have all the local and personal taste of 'scunnered', even if they are, in their way, translations.

So, for me, kvell and kvetch are words that not only have the meanings that I gave you with my translations. To me, they also express feelings from and about my parents and my first home. When I say 'kvell', I can see my father smiling. When I say 'kvetch', I can see my mother frowning. Even so, you can of course have those words and use them. That's what's great about language: it jumps the gaps and barriers between us.

We're on the hunt for good days. How might kvelling and kvetching help us? Should either of them ever be avoided? Can you overdo either or both of them? Can you 'overkvell' and 'overkvetch'?

Starting with kvell, as you've seen, my father spotted in my mother that she sometimes found it difficult to kvell. She was a very clever person, who overcame the low expectations of the time and place she lived in. She was that rare thing, a 'scholarship' girl, but in her family, living where they were, at that time, it was thought that the best thing she could do was be a secretary. So though she 'matriculated' at 16 and could have gone into the sixth form to do A-levels and go onto university, instead she went to secretarial college. It was only after I was born that she started getting more qualifications, teaching for a long time, then becoming a deputy head. Because we lived in an area where it was nigh on impossible for a woman to become a headteacher, she switched to becoming a lecturer at a teacher training college and started writing papers, articles and a book. The book was based on unique research, where she travelled all over the country observing teachers teaching, and talking to teachers about what they were trying to achieve through this or that method.

In the last years of her life, she was doing BBC Schools Radio programmes and giving lectures, sometimes for hundreds of people. But did she kvell? Nope. She found it hard to say to herself, 'I did well.' These days we've got the label 'impostor syndrome' and she did say to us that there were times when she thought she was in situations where everyone around her was 'cleverer' than she was. At other times, she felt that others weren't respecting her experience and what she was bringing to the table. Once or twice, I caught her crying with frustration at being sidelined, or finding that people were taking her ideas or materials and passing them off as their own, ruining them in the process. Or, as she put it to me, 'Michael, some people will turn even the best ideas to dreck' (poo).

I think in her heart of hearts she was proud of what she had done and what she had come through but that other side of her not-kvelling personality meant she thought it was wrong to kvell in public.

I've known others like Mum and I can see it makes them fed up. Even when there's a bit of paper, a certificate, a nationally acknowledged qualification saying, 'You have passed' or 'You are a qualified such-and-such', there's some last internal obstacle to your being wholeheartedly delighted about it.

Maybe there should be a Kvell School, where you go and learn how to be proud of what you've done. People talk a lot about what can motivate you, what can give you the oomph to go on and try. That other school, the School of Hard Knocks, says that you should keep telling people that they're not good enough. My wife sometimes watches those boot camp-type programmes where ordinary people put themselves through terrible outdoor challenges, pitting themselves against mountains, storms and each other, while being shouted at by 50-year-old men, yelling, 'You are a heap of fucking shit! What are you?' And the person – who has just run 500 miles up a glacier in bare feet – shouts back, 'I'm a heap of fucking shit, sir!' I can't stand these programmes. I hate the message that only by exposing yourself to the most challenging of conditions while being told you're useless will you discover your real self.

At my adult education Kvell School, people will talk about why and how they have come to think they're not good at things. The only rule in the place will be that no one can put anyone else down, least of all the teachers, all of whom will also talk about how they came to think they're not good at things. At Kvell School, people will only have to do things that they fancy doing and people can team up with whoever they want, whenever they want to do things in pairs or groups. Ideas of what people can do at Kvell School will depend on the 'skill set' of anyone and everyone there. There'll be a notice board where people put up what they can offer by way of teaching or play-leading or, yes, challenging. At the end of the day, people will have time to talk about how they think they did. This won't be a rule but kvelling will be encouraged. In fact, kvelling will be modelled by the teachers, showing how you can take pride in the smallest of things. It's what Americans call 'small wins', I think. You helped someone do something? Small win. Kvell time. You learned a new chord for the guitar? Small win. Kvell time. You remembered to take your pills without anyone reminding you? Small win. Kvell time. You got to understand the theory of relativity? It's a win. Kvell time.

Of course we know that uberkvelling is bloody annoying so there must be some kind of uberkvell detection system that helps us at Kvell School. It'll be to do with being on guard that people shouldn't use kvelling as a weapon, as a put-down to others. One way to get round that is to ensure that built into Kvell School is learning how to help others kvell. It's also possible that we might have to ban doing yourself down. It's what I call sawing your own legs off. If anyone hears anyone else sawing their legs off, you're allowed to do a sawing gesture and make sawing noises.

But of course Kvell School hasn't been built yet so we have to build Kvellology into our minds, often on our own. If we lose the art of kvelling, we lose days that could have been good days. A day that was full of good-day-ness that you didn't notice and didn't kvell about is a sad thing. It breaks my daughter's adage about being an optimistic nihilist: if there's nothing else out there, she said, we might as well make the most of what we've got here. Kvelling helps. And, in spite of what those crazy bullying TV programmes say, kvelling can help you go on having a go at things. Yes, it's true some people find that being 'constantly dissatisfied that what you've made is not quite as excellent as you thought it ought to be' is a motivation to try again, but such people are often both lucky and unhappy. The kind of days I'm on about in this book are about feeling good, not about feeling miserably supremely excellent.

Now to kvetching. Just to clear the decks on this: we all love kvetching but do you want to *be* a kvetch? You get the difference? Having a moan is great. It identifies what's bugging us, we share the minor irritations and hardships of life, like a rude neighbour and acid reflux, so we feel better. But are we someone who kvetches, or a kvetching person? The person who kvetches doesn't always kvetch. Someone like that knows how to use their kvetches so that they can feel good. The kvetching person is stuck in kvetchland. They are the kvetch. They can't get out of it. They kvetch all day, every day and it never cheers them up.

I'll grant you, it keeps them going, but at some expense to the life-spirit of others. I once lived in a street with two kvetches. One of them mixed kvetching with high anxiety. I once let on that I had done two years of a medical course but I did make clear that I was no good at it and got out. From that time on, this good lady would stop me in the street, and open a conversation straight away with things like, 'Feel my knee! Is that cancer?'

I'd say, 'Look I don't know. I'm not a doctor. And as far as I know there isn't something called knee cancer.'

'Oh, Michael,' she'd say, 'the baby doesn't sleep. That's where I've caught this thing, whatever it is. I'm glad it's not cancer.'

But then I'd say, 'Look, don't take my word for it. Go and see a doctor.'

And she'd say, 'So now you're saying it IS cancer?'

The other kvetch in the same street was at least 99 years old. She would also stop me in the street and start the same conversation that she had started yesterday, the week before and every time I ever met her.

'... I was on the buses, you know? It was during the war, you see. The men was away so we women used to do the work. Do you know Pedro Street over there?'

'Yes,' I'd say.

She'd carry on: 'When the bomb dropped, you could hear all the knockers on the houses going rap, rap, rap, rap, rap all down the street.'

That was to get my attention. It always worked. I liked hearing those stories, but it was a con.

It was just to get me to stand still so that she could get kvetching about 'him upstairs'. 'He's driving me mad, Michael,' she'd say, 'him and his music. He's tapping the floor. I tell him. "You're tapping the bleeding floor," I says to him. But does he stop? Nah. If you see him, promise me this: tell him to stop tapping on the bleeding floor.'

That's it. I don't think that over several years I ever had any other conversation with her. At least with the hypochondriac, the conditions changed each week. They were both in their own ways finding it difficult to have good days.

I'm no psychologist but perhaps they had never had a chance to kvell about very much, though the older one was proud of having been on the buses, and quite rightly so. Perhaps it was the way the post-war world sidelined her that left her with just that to hang on to. And now she felt disrespected by the man upstairs.

And because neither of them had been to my Kvell School, neither of them had learned my One Small Thing Principle. How does that work? Quite often it's my job in the house to scrub the oven pans. As you'll know from E is for Experiment,

I was an apprentice washer-upper from the age of six in the Harold and Connie Rosen Family School of Domestic Chores. Now, cleaning oven pans can be annoying, irritating and frustrating. The job is full of kvetch potential. You can spend as much time kvetching about it as actually cleaning the pans.

But no.

The One Small Thing Principle tells you that if you find a new technique or you successfully apply an old technique and either of these gets the burnt crud out of the corner, or degreases under the lip, then that's a win. Thus, listen up – we have a square sink. I figured out, all on my own, without help from anyone else, that I could jam the resistant oven pan into the corner of the sink, and work pressure with my frizzer on the troublesome corner crud. Result. Win. Kvell.

And, as you'll see in N is for Nights, we take that kvell to bed with us, where, as Shakespeare said, it rounds the day with a little sleep. Or something like that.

Btw, this book doesn't have enough dad jokes.

What do you call it when Dad moans he can't get the sauce out the bottle?

Tomato kvetchup.

SUGGESTION

Obviously my idea of a Kvell School is a fantasy, but is there a realistic way in which we can school ourselves to a) talk about bad stuff without putting each other down and b) celebrate the good stuff? Maybe calling it the Kvell School is a useful way to put this in the front of our minds.

L

is for Little by Little

Depending on your taste, you may know that phrase as a song – different songs, same title – by Junior Wells, the Rolling Stones or Dusty Springfield, and there are others. Mostly these songs are about losing someone, little by little, which is not quite what I'm talking about here. Instead of something dissolving, I'm thinking of growing and building.

Some people are either so hugely talented or so hugely lucky, that they can think big and do big. To be honest, I envy them. I imagine that these are the folk who write 500-page novels, direct epic movies, design sports stadiums, plan cities, take over other people's countries. (OK, I don't envy people taking over other people's countries!) I'm guessing that they get to 'big' by doing little by little first. I don't know for sure. What I do know is that if you're after feeling good in a day, or day by day, then little by little is a helpful way to think. It's of course a very similar idea to 'a journey of a thousand miles begins with a single step', a quotation from Chapter 64 of the *Tao Te Ching* ascribed to Laozi.

Here's an example. Not long ago, someone came to me with what sounded like a good idea. It was for a story. It was a big story and quite complicated. There were things that you could do in the story. I mean that there were things that you could learn how to do, as you read the story. (I can't tell you what these were, in case I give it away.) When I read the idea, I could 'see' it. I saw it straightaway as a big thing. I saw it as a book or a TV programme. I saw TV presenters telling it and doing it.

That's the vision. Many of us have visions like this. We see the big thing. That's fine but, I would say, it won't happen unless you also think little by little. One moment at a time, one scene at a time. As you do these little things, it may well be necessary to hold the vision in mind, as if you're making a mosaic. You put one tiny tile down at a time to make the big picture.

When you do little by little, it's obvious that you might not finish in a day. What follows from this is that you have to both take pleasure in what you've done that day, and yet give yourself the oomph to carry on tomorrow (or whenever you've got the time to pick up again). If I think of me writing something, it may be that I finish a poem or a newspaper article or a radio script in a day. That's great. It may be, though, that I'm writing something longer, a story, a talk for my university, the PhD I did (it took three years), or this book (!). I know before I start that I'm not going to finish it in a day. This means I've got to keep being positive even though, day after day, it's unfinished. I'm not going to lie about this: this is not easy. There are always reasons to not carry on: I've lost my train of thought; it's feeling samey, so I'm getting bored; I'll never finish; I'm going to eat some cake; what's on the telly?; there's that story I was going to write, I could start that instead; I wonder who Arsenal are going to buy in the transfer window …

These are all fine, and after I've been at the thing I'm doing, any of these are great ways to take a break. But how do I carry on? How do I persevere, see it through? I sing 'Little by little' (usually the Stones' version without going into the stuff about 'losin' my lerve for yoooo'. Or I extend the Dusty Springfield one by singing 'Little by little by little by little by little by little by little …' on and on, as if I'm climbing a huge ladder). Hey! There's a thought: a ladder is another good image for what I'm talking about here. You can't go up a whole ladder in one step. You have to go rung by rung. In other words, I have to drum into my head that the thing I'm doing is made out of little steps AND if I keep on doing these little things, it will eventually become the bigger thing.

So this has become about finishing, completing, getting it done. Many of us are great at starting things, but we're also really good at not-finishing. Some people have turned not-finishing into an art form. At one level, this doesn't matter. You can have a lot of fun never finishing. But if it makes you unhappy, if you start to hate yourself because nothing ever gets done, there's a problem. Bad days.

The good thing about singing 'Little by Little' is that it reminds me of how to finish. Think of the Rolling Stones. In one sense they are huge. They have a huge song list. They've sold millions of records. They play huge stadiums. They are hugely popular. But it's all been done little by little. One chord at a time. One phrase at a time. One song at a time. One gig at a time. For more than 60 years they've been finishing stuff. Stuff gets done. And yet, even they would say, sometimes some of it wasn't much good. A song didn't work, a gig fell apart. So they did another little thing. Then another. Then another.

I can see that it may seem absurd to measure yourself against one of the most successful showbiz acts of all time. Obviously, we aren't all going to become one of the most successful showbiz acts of all time. But it's not the success I'm talking about. It's the method of doing little by little in order to get something done. Why? Because ultimately, to feel good, getting the thing done, does it. Well, it does it for me!

My daughter sometimes cooks treats. From the time she was quite young, she learned how to bake muffins and buns. Classic little by little stuff. You make a mix, you make one bun at a time. You serve them up. We eat them one bun at a time. We say, 'Yum!' Gratification all round. Goal scored! She started off with cake mixes from the supermarket. To be absolutely honest, the results weren't great. If a cake hasn't got raisins in, I don't see the point. But of course, I didn't say that. Not at all. It was: 'This is wonderful' and 'Yum!'

Then over the years she's branched out, she's improvised. Sometimes this has worked, sometimes it hasn't. Each time, it's little by little. In the process, she's found which ones are our favourites. For this last Christmas, my Christmas present was a tray of apple, cinnamon and raisin muffins. It was wonderful. Totally perfect in every way. I could say from the bottom of my heart, in all honesty, that they were great. It was a superb Christmas present. And the point here was that for it to be a present, it had to be finished. In my mind, if not in hers, there were hundreds of days over what must be ten years or more, of little by littles, lying behind that one Christmas present.

If I talk about writing or cooking, or producing songs, then finishing is important, maybe necessary for a good day. In those examples, there is a vision, there are end points in view: the talk to be given, the cake to be cooked, the record to make, the script to be recorded, the gig to be played and so on. But there is another way to do little by little. It's more like, let's see what happens. More tentative, more suck it and see. It's like taking your pen for a walk to see what it's going to say.

On these occasions, you don't have the vision. You just get into the thing. You go to the cupboard and pull out the chunky piccalilli pickle and the hummus and see if they'll go together. You go to your keyboard and just start typing any old stuff that jumps into your mind. You sit at a piano keyboard and play notes to see what pops up. I've partly talked about this already in C is for Curiosity, but this is even freer than that. You might not even be asking curiosity questions. It's more that you're sitting with whatever it is you like doing, and just seeing what crops up as you start on it.

Here's another example: I have to do a lot of stretching to make sure that my hamstrings don't tighten up. I've looked online at American guys in tight T-shirts saying, 'Hey if you've got tight hamstrings, then I've got this great exercise that Chuck and I are going to show you …' I've looked at books. I've listened to my offspring tell me what they've done at the gym and what their physios (!) have told them to do. I try them. They're good. And you can only do stretching exercises one at a time, little by little. But, here's the point, I find that I don't have to do them in exactly the way they tell me to. Warning: whatever I do, I do it gently, but I can improv little stretches, just like you can improv a dance. So, to be clear, this isn't about creating new, rigorous, painful moves. Far, far from it. This is about gently extending or bending or reaching. It's like dancing slowly. Little by little. Getting it done.

Knowledge comes into this, too. Let's go back to the Rolling Stones. When they were, let's say, 11 years old, they didn't know very much about the blues, rock 'n' roll, gospel, rhythm 'n' blues, soul and Tamla Motown. By the time they produced their first album, when they were in their twenties and as they got into their thirties, they knew an enormous amount. How come?

They immersed themselves in recordings, going to gigs and playing. Step by step, little by little, they built up a huge knowledge of these different forms, different musics, different ways of playing, different ways of working. It was all knowledge. We often think of knowledge as always or inevitably attached to schools, exams and colleges. This is true, but if we say that that's the only place where we can find it, we can diminish the knowledges that we can build at home, with our friends or anywhere away from the knowledge centres and knowledge factories in education.

From the Stones to my daughter. She built that knowledge up, step by step, little by little, sometimes using recipes, sometimes adapting them, sometimes starting with, 'I wonder if this or that will work ...'

Or it can be a mix of both education and home. I give myself as an example here. I've done so much education in my life, I sometimes think that I've spent more time in education than I've spent anywhere else apart from home. Education is coming out of my ears. I've read stuff, analysed stuff, analysed the analyses, taught the stuff, taught the analyses, taught the analyses of the analyses, analysed what I've taught ... I love it.

In all that time, I've written. And because most of what I've been doing in education is to do with writing, I've learned a lot about writing in education. But having said that, I've also had to learn outside of these places of learning how to do little by little, how to do step by step and how to take risks, how to improv, how to suck it and see. And by doing that, I've learned new things that I didn't learn in the places of learning.

One example: in May 2025, Sir Keir Starmer made a speech about immigration. He used the phrase 'an island of strangers'. I found myself reacting to this. It felt insulting and hostile, and straight away I was thinking about my spell in hospital, when 'strangers' looked after me. In my head I ran through how they'd cared for me and saved my life, day by day, little by little, and I also remembered where many of the doctors, nurses and health workers came from. So I 'wrote' this in my head:

I lay in bed
hardly able to breathe
but there were people to sedate me,
pump air into me
calm me down when I thrashed around
hold my hand and reassure me
play me songs my family sent in
turn me over to help my lungs
shave me, wash me, feed me
check my medication
perform the tracheostomy
people on this 'island of strangers'
from China, Jamaica, Brazil, Ireland
India, USA, Nigeria and Greece.

I sat on the edge of my bed
and four people came with
a frame and supported me
or took me to a gym
where they taught me how
to walk between parallel bars
or kick a balloon
sat me in a wheel chair
taught me how to use the exercise bike
how to walk with a stick
how to walk without a stick
people on this 'island of strangers'

from China, Jamaica, Brazil, Ireland
India, USA, Nigeria and Greece.

If ever you're in need as I was
may you have an island of strangers
like I had.

SUGGESTION

Can you make up a poem in your head? Try a limerick.
Try a simple four-line type like this one of mine:

Down behind the dustbin
I met a dog called Jim.
He didn't know me
I didn't know him.

This type means that you think up one half and 'throw'
it at the other half, making the two halves rhyme.

If you can rap (or any other rhyming form like that
– calypso, folk song, shanty, etc.), see if you can make up
one in your head.

If it's easier to do with an instrument, do it that way.

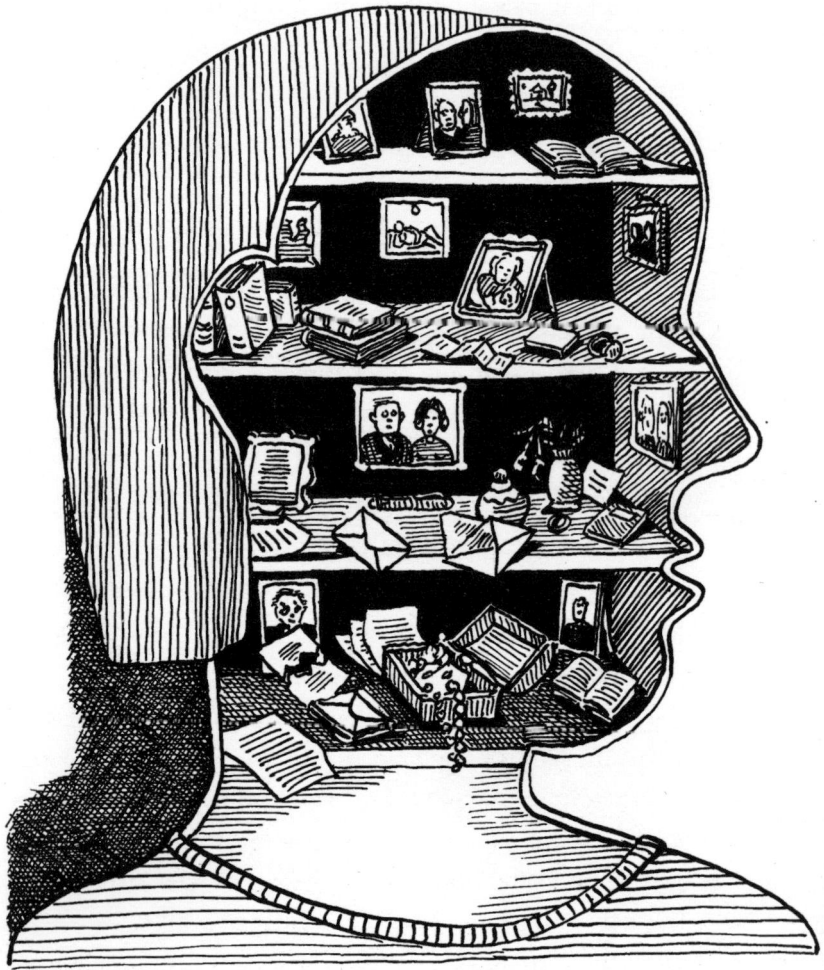

M

is for Memory

I've had great memory days. I don't mean days when I've done things that have turned out to be great memories. And I don't mean days when I've sat and thought through some great memories. What I mean is when something has turned up which stores a memory – things like letters or diaries, photos or any kind of object or memento. And then, how these are part of a dot-to-dot picture, linking moments, memories and events.

An example: my cousins and I have been writing to each other for many years, sometimes quizzing each other about memories or glimpses of relatives we share. Out of the blue, one of my second cousins in America told me that he had strong memories of the man I would have called Grandpa or 'Zeyde' (Yiddish), if I had ever known him. He was the Polish-American father of my father, but the last time my father saw him was when he was two. Morris (that was his name) didn't ever follow my father's mother, Rose, and the three of their five children to London. In that sense, for all the relatives over here in England, Morris is a blank, just a name and some photos. But over there in the States, there were, and still are, people who knew him – like my father's cousin Ted.

I sat in the 'den' in Ted's house when he was in his eighties and nineties and even when he was 101, listening to stories about Morris. How Morris was an orator and spoke at meetings, how Morris used to arrive at the house with a trunk full of five suits. How Morris wore spats. How Morris once turned up at the house with a 'convertible' but Ted's mother wouldn't ride with Morris in the convertible on account of Morris having an 'illegitimate child'. How on the day when Morris and Rose split, and Rose left for the train, their two oldest sons, Sydney and Laurence, were hoeing in the field and they didn't even say goodbye to each other. Rose and my father never saw Sydney again and they only saw Laurence twice more before he died when he was 21.

As for that 'illegitimate child' – well, after Ted died at 103 (followed later by his wife Gladys), Ted's son Teddy went into the house and opened a 'closet'. In the closet was a sealed box, marked 'Family Photos'. In the box was a set of photos of the relatives in France and Poland who had been killed in the Holocaust: relatives who had only ever been spoken of, never looked at – Martin, Oscar (also known as Jeschie), Lucie-Thérèse, Rachel, Stella, Bella, Mishke ('Michael') and others none of us can name. On the bottom of the pile was a picture of a baby boy ('13 mths old') and on the back was the name Ira Gerald Kane and an address, '365 Powers Ave, Bx' [Bronx, New York]. Then it says, 'Parents, Mr and Mrs Theodore Kane'.

Was this the 'illegitimate child' – Morris's son, my father's half-brother? Was this child the subject of the story that Ted told me when he was 90, about how Morris had once come to him with his wallet, flipped it open and shown him a picture of a boy and had said to Ted, 'Do you think this kid is smart?' When Ted (then a teenager) had shrugged, Morris put the picture away. Even so, even then, when Ted was in his nineties, he didn't ever say in words that this boy was 'illegitimate'. It took Ted till he was 101 to tell me that. I'm not sure why he waited that long. Had he thought that I shouldn't know? This was, after all, about stuff that went on in the 1920s and here we were in the twenty-first century. Oh yes, Ted said, and another thing. 'When Morris showed me the picture, he said that kid was his landlady's kid.'

But given that it was such a big deal about telling me this stuff in dribs and drabs, Teddy and I set about tracing Ira Gerald Kane.

After several months, we finally got to Ira Gerald Kane's grandsons – who, as it happens, were in and around Reno in Nevada but not talking to each other. We hit them with the news that Teddy and I could be their relatives. There were stories about Mr and Mrs Theodore Kane not getting on too well and Mr Kane being out on the road quite often. It was all falling into place ... the sometimes itinerant Morris Rosen staying at the house, while he was on the road doing trade union business on the Eastern Seaboard? All of a sudden I've got new American relatives?

All we had to do was some DNA testing to confirm it. We did. And there was no match. The whole thing had been a wild goose chase. Or was it?

Had we stumbled across a strange and pathetic story in which Morris thought (or was told) that he was father to a child (a lovely-looking boy, by the way!), was ostracised by his sister-in-law and others for being the father of an 'illegitimate child' but, in actual fact, he was no such thing?

After all, there was no other link between the Rosen family in Massachusetts and the Kane family in Nevada. The only known reason as to why this photo of a baby boy should be 'hiding' under photos (which were also long hidden) of Rosens killed in the Holocaust, was that Morris had, it seemed, an 'illegitimate child' and yet, the DNA said no! Had Morris supported this child believing it was his? We don't know.

There's one more bit. There's also cousin Howard, related to me through Ted's sister Olga. (It was Olga, by the way, who told me that she couldn't tell me anything about the relatives who disappeared in the Holocaust, but long after she was gone, I found online a letter she had sent to the US immigration authorities asking whether she could bring Oscar – 'Jeschie' – Rosen to the US. Why couldn't she have told me that when I met her? I don't have an answer to that.) Anyway, her son Howard is in America too and he told me that he remembered Morris from when he (Howard) was very young. Morris, he said, called him 'little pisher' – literally 'little pisser' but in this context not meant at all disparagingly!

A tiny thing. A single word. 'Pisher'. A bit of Yiddish slang, brought over from Poland on a boat in 1912, stuck onto a child and now being repeated in 2023 – a memory of a man, a grandfather to me, but someone I never knew, never saw, someone my father never knew beyond the age of two. The word cuts through the decades and seems more alive than all the bits of paper I've dug up to do with the elusive Morris – things like the election he fought in 1928 as a candidate for the Pennsylvania Senate or the speech he gave at the Boot and Shoe Workers' Union Congress in 1922 calling for Eugene Debs to be released from jail on account of his opposition to the First World War.

'Little pisher' is more tangible even than the gravestone I found in the Jewish Workmen's Circle Cemetery in Melrose, Boston. There he sits, Morris Rosen, 'beloved father' (beloved father? By which children? Really?), 'son of Jonas', two engraved hands clasping each other, the symbol of the Jewish Workmen's Circle, along with the Workmen's Circle branch number. I looked it up. It was Mattapan, a district in Boston.

But also in that district was what Ted talked of as 'Boston's largest mental institution'. Yes, in his last years, Morris was institutionalised. Did Ted go to see him in there? I asked. 'My father,' Ted said, speaking of Morris's brother here, 'said that Morris's condition had so deteriorated that there wasn't much point in going to see him.'

By 1950 (when this was going on), Ted was a doctor, so it seemed strange that he didn't go to see his uncle Morris in Boston's biggest mental institution. Years later I found out that at this time, the 'Mattapan' (as the institution was known locally) was experimenting with lobotomies. Had Morris ended his life in a stupor brought on by having his brain cut? I've tried to find out. I've sent pleading letters to authorities who pass the letters on to other authorities but in the end I get a letter explaining that they can't or won't or shouldn't tell me anything. Quite who or what they think they are defending by not telling me, I don't know. This is an example of 'them' holding a memory. I'm not allowed to get at it or into it.

So this is a set of interlocking stories, some oral, some written, some embedded in public records, trade union congresses, election lists, some on photos and on the backs of photos, some on Nazi deportation records: seemingly endless lines linking together people scattered between Poland, France, England and the US; some lines ending in cul-de-sacs, like zero-matching DNA tests. Every now and then Ancestry adds a detail too: Morris's draft card for the First World War, telling me the name of his birthplace, a village near Warsaw, Krośniewice. I bring up Google Street View and stare at the pictures of the houses and town hall. What do I think I'll find in them? The ghost of Morris Rosen? I imagine that perhaps in the town hall, they have a record of Morris Rosen being born or of his parents, Jonas and Marta, getting married. I think of talking to one of our Polish friends and asking her to help me write a letter to the Krośniewice Town Hall. And then I think, maybe not. I come back to Howard and Morris calling him 'little pisher'. That'll do for the time being.

Well, yes and no. What about my father? What did he think of the father he never knew? His sister Sylvia told me that

Morris was always going to come to London but he never did. For a while he used to send Sylvia cards and toys. For some reason he didn't send any to my father, who was nearly four years younger than Sylvia.

There was something else. Rose came from the US with three children: Sylvia, my father and a baby boy, Wallace. But baby Wallace died soon after getting here and, it seems, Morris blamed Rose for his death. I remember Rose. Long dark dress, dark coat – always, always in a hat. Talking with my father about politics. Diving into her huge black bag and fishing out a red shoehorn. 'Here,' she said, 'it's for you.' I didn't know then that Morris had blamed her for the death of Wallace. Or that Rose and the children always thought that one day Morris would arrive. In fact, my father had always nursed this dream when things got noisy and nasty in the two-up, two-down house packed with 10 (or was it 11?) people, with Rose being blamed for not being able to hang on to her husband, Rose who always thought she was a cut above the rest with her fancy ideas about books and politics, and not giving the boy (my father) a bar mitzvah, like all the other boys, small wonder his uncle didn't make him the suit. Rose it was who'd had polio so that if she worked in a shop or as a secretary, she could only work one-handed. And here she was landing up in this tiny house as if it wasn't full up anyway … but, my father fantasised, one day his dad, Morris Rosen, would arrive from America, and take him away from all this hectic, uncomfortable stuff. Or so he dreamed.

And then, my father once told me, 'Ma' (as he called her, hanging on to a remnant of his American babyhood) would have to go into hospital. So, who was looking after him when she was away, I wondered? Well, there was his formidable 'bubbe' (grandma) who cooked and cooked and cooked, it seems. She cooked things, which, if my father mentioned them at teatime, took on the life of the feasts of fiction (remember the cholent in G is for Grounded?). 'Ah,' he'd say, 'no one ever made prunes like my bubbe did.' What? *A prune is a prune is a prune*, I thought. I only ate them because Mum said that they kept me 'regular'. 'Giant prunes,' he would say with a look on his face as if envisaging a lost heaven, but here now, tragically and awfully, we were in exile in the suburbs, cut off from Bubbe's giant prunes. Mum would be infuriated but bit her lip.

My brother and I would keep our heads down. This was deep stuff to do with a place and time way, way back in that mythic land called 'The Thirties' and 'The East End' (of London). We never went there. There were no pictures of it. Anyone we knew who once lived there or then had 'moved out'. All that was left there were giant prunes and cholent.

But Bubbe was old. If Rose was in hospital and died, Bubbe would be too old, surely. What about Rose's sisters? Well, they were the ones who shouted at Rose and told her that she was too good for her own good. Though Auntie Hilda and Uncle Alf, who didn't have children of their own, always said that they would look after him. But the problem with Auntie Hilda was that she ran a clothes stall on Hoxton Market and he had to sit under the stall all day, watching the jellied-eels man on the other side of the street, chopping up live eels. Chop chop chop chop, and then taking his knife and swooshing the pieces off the chopping board into the bucket. Slooosh.

Alf and Hilda, my father said to me one day, left me their silver Kiddush cups. 'Here, you have them,' he said to me one day. What with him and Rose having been communists, he didn't pass on the vital bit of information on what a Kiddush cup is. In fact, I wasn't as ignorant as I thought I was, because even though my parents didn't welcome in 'shabbes' (the sabbath) with a prayer and a meal, some of my friends did. I had even been offered a drink from a Kiddush cup many times over at Dave's house by his father Morris (another Morris!) but that, Dave's mother said, was one of Morris's jokes. So when my father said they were Auntie Hilda's and Uncle Alf's Kiddush cups, I didn't remember Dave's dad calling it a Kiddush cup. He just kept on filling it with wine and telling us that he wasn't allowed to give me any after all.

So what would my father do, if his mother died? There was one other person: there was 'Zeyde' (Grandpa). He was from the 'heim' (Yiddish for home or homeland, in this case). My father always made it seem that he loved Zeyde, with his floppy moustache, his accent, getting little Harold (my father) to read him the newspaper because he found it too hard, promising to make him the bar mitzvah suit to make up for the bar mitzvah suit Harold didn't get because he didn't have a bar mitzvah. One time I was standing in the Arsenal sports shop, buying an Arsenal shirt for my son, when a young man I had never seen before, standing next to me, but not looking at me, said, 'I'm sorry that my great-grandfather didn't make your dad a bar mitzvah suit.' What? Who said that? Oh, it's this guy buying Arsenal gear. I said to him, while not looking at him, and while studying the new Arsenal away kit, 'It's OK, his zeyde made one for him anyway.' It turned out to be my third cousin once removed.

My brother and I swap these stories and they travel out to cousins and second cousins and then stories flow back. Out of the blue, not long before she died, my cousin, the daughter of Harold's sister Sylvia (Gillian) said that she had found a letter. She sent me a copy of it.

This is what it said:

Dear Mummy
    I hope you have noticed that I can do writing. I will show you by the next word. I hope you soon be out.

Friday was Pearly's <u>Birthday</u> but she's having her party on <u>saturday</u>. I hope you recived the <u>Birtday card</u> she sent you. Please send me an answer, your loving son Harold kisses from all the family xxxxxxxxxxxxxxxxxxxxxxxxxxxxxxx xxxxxxxxxxxxxxxxxxxxxxxxxxxxxxx

[spellings and punctuation not corrected]

Yet another fragment from the past, stored away for decades, suddenly and unexpectedly surfacing. Now that I've written here where my father was at, at around the time he was sending this to Rose in the London Hospital, you can see behind this letter (written when my father was about six or seven I would guess), all the worries and losses and mysteries that he was carrying with him. 'I hope you soon be out,' he tells her. 'Please send me an answer,' he pleads. And he sends 'kisses from all the family' but did he know that some of them were cross with Rose? Did they really send their kisses?

One other thing: my father wrote a lot in his life. It's in files, pamphlets, articles, books. There are poems, stories, polemical articles about education and handwritten notes that his second wife Betty has brought me, and even a poem written on the birth of my first child, Joe, reflecting on holding him but apologising to Joe for thinking of his wife (my mum) who died just before he was born. But he didn't ever mention this letter and, for all I know, he forgot that he had ever sent it. It only survived because Rose must have given it to Sylvia, because Sylvia left it for her daughter Gillian and because Gillian sent it to me.

These survivals matter. They are treasures. It was only because my second cousin's mother's brother in America (!) kept four letters from Poland and France, that I could ever find out what happened to the relatives who were killed in the Holocaust. No survival story, though, for the chest full of letters that my father sent to Mum during his time in Frankfurt and Berlin in 1945, 1946 and 1947 while he was in the US Army. They were there in the chest all through my childhood. They were there in the first house we moved to. They were there in the second house we moved to. But by the time he moved again, they were gone.

As I'm writing these words that you're reading now, that chest is less than a yard away from my left foot. That's because my father made that chest himself. I may not have the letters (what a pity I didn't read them one time of the many times I saw them), but every joint and hinge on the chest, he made.

That's a different kind of memory.

So living with and in memories is a great way to have a good day.

SUGGESTION

Do you have relatives who've got stuff 'tidied away' that you've never seen? If you ask them, might they show you? If they show you, can you record them on your phone talking about it? Can you take pics of the documents or photos they show you?

Are there boxes that you've never opened? Why's that? Is it because it's too painful or you fear what's in them? Is now the time to open them? If you have reached that point, might it be a good idea to open them with a sister, brother, spouse or best friend as company? If you've got the box or boxes, why have you got them, if you won't open them?

N

is for Nights

I guess this is an irony: a chapter on nights in a book about days. But there's a good reason for it. If our nights are crap, our days are crap. We're irritable and ineffective. We find it hard to concentrate, hard to remember stuff, hard to relax, hard to think, hard to be nice to anyone, more likely to fly off the handle. And that's just the stuff we can see and be aware of. We can be pretty sure that all the parts of our body that need to rest in order to recuperate, repair and regenerate are having a hard time, too.

I have one big insight into this. In 2020, I was put into an induced coma. It lasted for around 42 days. While I was put into this coma, I was intubated and ventilated – meaning that the doctors and nurses put a tube down my throat and pumped air down the tube into my lungs.

But why did they do that? The theory behind it is that if you 'switch off' a patient then you give them a better chance of recovery. Imagine the picture: someone in this situation is lying on their back, hardly moving any part of their body. The main movement is coming from the air being pumped into their chest. I'm told it's quite violent. The chest heaves up and down. The patient isn't even making the effort themselves to do what it takes to breathe, which involves – amongst other things – the diaphragm, the intercostal muscles (the ones between your ribs) and many of the muscles around your mouth, nose, tongue and throat.

The theory behind this kind of procedure is that because the patient doesn't do that stuff for themselves, the regenerative powers that the body has are not in any way 'competing' with the muscles and nerves of the body for energy and power.

Just to be clear, it's a last-ditch, last-resort procedure, when all else has failed or is failing. In the case of a virus (as in my case, with Covid), antibiotics don't work, so the body has to rely on its own cells to eliminate or diminish the virus.

But of course, only a tiny, tiny minority of us ever have this kind of treatment and of those who receive it, not all (far from it) survive. The rest of us are dealing with viruses and bacteria on our own at home using medicines that relieve the effects (painkillers and the like) or, in the case of bacteria, antibiotics.

Any doctor will tell you that one of the best treatments for illness is rest and sleep. We all know that if we try to ignore heavy colds, flu, or any other big infection like bronchitis or pneumonia, our bodies can't cope. Things get worse. Purely anecdotally, I know of examples of people who worked through heavy colds and got much more serious infections. It's as if viruses and bacteria are opportunistic and thrive when the body they're in is not resting.

Perhaps you know all this like you know how to breathe – though I get the impression that some people know it but ignore it, while others know it but can't stop work because they'll lose pay or 'the work' (whatever it is) won't get done.

It follows, then, that if our sleep time is at night then nights are our place of healing. Nights are our rehab treatment. If we can't sleep, it's more difficult to rehab. (The opposite is true, too: if we can't rehab, it's difficult to sleep.) I know this stuff from my time in a rehab hospital which happened when I came out of the induced coma. It was an incredible, awakening time for me, in which I discovered a lot about myself and a lot about the people who know how to rehabilitate us. I learned that the people looking after me were helping me to help myself. It wasn't an easy thing to learn or to accept. It's much easier to sit back and hope that the people in uniforms would help me do everything. But that doesn't do the job. You have to use what they say and do in order to help yourself. Much of the time, I was in a strange state of flux in which I thought I knew what was going on, but the next day, realised that the day before I hadn't known what was going on. This was unsettling and troubling. There were times when I lay in bed at night not knowing why I was there, what was going on or whether I would ever get better again. Starting out from the time I was in the ward in the ordinary hospital and then through the three weeks in rehab, some of the nights were long, strange, eerie, lonely, worrying and bewildering.

To start off with, I was mildly delirious (very lucky not to be hallucinating, actually) and I would have ludicrous fantasies about what I would or could or should do. I called my wife in the middle of the night and said, 'I could come home.' Very patiently, she told me that I had to take it easy, do the exercises, and I would get better. When we ended the call, I lay there sweating, imagining that I'd be stuck in hospital forever. At that very moment, there was one night shift group that came on who for some reason took a strange delight in having a laugh at my expense. They wouldn't let me have the buzzer which I was desperate to have in case I wet myself or soiled myself – a real possibility at the time because I was still incapacitated.

I'm telling this story as a typical example of how nights can multiply our anxieties, fill our minds full of situations that seem intractable, impossible to solve. We twist and turn. We sweat. We itch. When we think of solutions, for some reason, we think up the worst – the least practical, the least feasible and the downright daft. How could I have come home? I couldn't even stand up!

Into the midst of this, every noise, every change in atmosphere is magnified and seems at the time to last forever, hour after hour. The sound of monitors, drips, feeds and any bit of apparatus beeped and bopped nearby, in the middle distance and far off. Other patients' snoring, sniffing, breathing, coughing, scratching, tapping, talking, groaning was relentless. Every light in the ward or outside in the street seemed to be shining right into my eyes – which, as it happens, I was told are rather peculiar because they don't close! My eyes protrude and when I doze or sleep, the eyelids can't be bothered to shut.

I'm saying all this because what happened then is an extreme form of what happens to many of us at home when we become hyperaware of our surroundings when we can't sleep. Clocks ticking, foxes screaming, cats scratching, streetlights shining through blinds, partners breathing or (of course) snoring.

And we seem to be so awake. Much more awake than when, during the day, after nights like this, we're trying to be awake and alert and yet feel tired! It's a vicious pendulum – all eyes and ears at night, all dull and dozy during the day.

And there is always so much to be worried about: work, bills, people who've said things that you wished you had replied to, regrets that you can do nothing about, impending disasters, risks that you don't know whether you could or should take, plans that are bound to go wrong, an imagined repeat of a hellish thing that happened last time, an offence you think you may have caused, a dead end you can't get out of, the thing you wish you had said, an undefined fear or anger that you dare not speak about … and on and on it goes …

Question: is it possible to sleep with any or all of this stuff, outside or inside, going on? I'm going to stick my neck out and say yes. And say further: if you don't sleep, whatever it is that's bothering you will get worse. Lack of sleep makes nearly everything worse.

So it may well be that any or all of the things I've mentioned are real and necessary problems that have to be solved, situations that have to be relieved. The question, though, is whether it's possible to delay solving and relieving them by putting in some time to 'flake out' (as my dad used to call it), have a kip, get a good sleep.

Here are my tricks. I'm not going to claim that they're absolutely failsafe and whatever I'm suggesting, you may want to adapt so that it works for you. Remember the principle: whatever works, works!

First step is the 'one good thing' principle. At some point, at the beginning, on your way to bed, as you get into bed, as your head hits the pillow, you concentrate on one good thing that happened to you, or that you did on that day. It can be as tiny and as insignificant as how you successfully washed a burnt, greased-up oven pan! Or how you bought a really good new pen! Anything that involved sorting or cleaning or new is good. The best time to do this, I find, is exactly at the moment I close my eyes. The trick is to really concentrate on the memory of this one good thing. Concentrating on this one good thing seems to have the effect of pushing away the bad stuff that's going to bother you later.

Now for the next step.

The core method here is to bore myself to sleep. The thing about all those worries and external irritations that I've mentioned, is that they all become really interesting. Obsessively so. You find yourself dwelling on them and that leads to you concentrating on them instead of sleeping. So you've got to do something that is so boring that your brain gets fed up and switches off.

My failsafe bore is counting, starting at one. But that's not enough. It's not any old counting. You have to count slowly, concentrating on each number, thinking of the shape of the number itself. However, you won't be able to. Your mind wants to be interested in all that other stuff. So by the time you get to about nine or ten, your mind flips onto one of the anxieties or terrors. What do you do now? You go back to one. What? But that's sooooo boring! Exactly. You start again. Slowly, carefully, thinking of the shape of each number. The moment that your mind flicks onto one of the anxieties, back you go to one.

Word of warning: you don't do this in an irritated way. You do it in a detached, calm and contented way. You don't even say to yourself 'back to one' because that's another subject in itself. You just go back to one, gently, nonchalantly, calmly.

The first night you do this, it may be really hard and frustrating. Don't forget that part of you loves to get into those hateful cycles of panic, fear and terror, and your mind actually resents the fact that you're trying to lock them out and switch them off. You might at some time of the day visualise this: fears and irritations trying to get in through your window and you pushing them away with numbers. Don't think of that image when you're counting because the whole point of the counting is that it must be only counting. It must be deadly, deadly boring.

Now there are one or two other disciplines that you have to do alongside this. You must not, must not, move, twitch, fiddle, scratch, rub, shift about in any way. You are a statue. Think of yourself as a statue. Alongside this deadly boring counting, you must be absolutely and boringly still. Now here's the extra tricky bit: if you do twitch, scratch, shake your leg or some such, back you go to one. Again, don't do it resentfully or irritatedly. Just do it nonchalantly and calmly. If you have an intolerable itch or throat catch or some such, just do it, then start again. When you start again, always try to do it without a thought or narrative, just bring up that number one and start counting.

So you have two things going on here: counting and being a statue.

Now there are some more tricks. Before you start this routine, you may want to try some gentle – and it must, must be gentle – stretching. And probably not an overall body stretch. It may be just your feet and lower legs. Or it may be your chest. Any part of you that feels a bit knotty, a bit tied up. Think of this kind of stretch as a relaxer, not an exertion.

Something else – and some people find that this is the game-changer rather than the counting: the breathing. Before you get into the counting routine, you can try a breathing routine. The best one is to breathe in through your nose to the count of three or four. Hold it for one or two and breathe out gently through your mouth for three or four. In this pre-counting stage (!), you may want to breathe out through pursed lips, as if you are gently doing what it takes to blow a trumpet. What this does is make your diaphragm work. It also flattens the base of your back, where at the end of a day there may well be tension and aches. Big thing here: you must concentrate on the breathing. Do the breath-counting and be aware of what the breathing is doing to your body: to your back and your chest. It may even make your toes or fingertips tingle because it's improving your circulation. Don't 'do' anything. Just feel it. Stay as still as you can, apart from what you need to do to do the breathing. For some people, this breathing is boring enough to send you off to sleep anyway. If after a good spell of doing it, you're still awake, it's time to bring in the counting.

One more thing: your neck and shoulders. For whatever reason, we humans seem to hunch and scrunch our necks and shoulders when we talk, when we write, when we read, when we pore over our phones and computers, when we get into arguments, when we sit on buses and get cross because the bus is late or we get stuck in a traffic jam. I am one of the world's worst neck and shoulder scrunchers. I also poke my head forwards like a chicken, pulling on my neck. When you get into bed, before you start on the counting, you might want to try to do something about this scrunching and hunching.

This is not easy to do entirely on your own. While you do the breathing (or before you do it; after all, you can't do everything at once!), you might want to see if you can relieve your neck of the weight of your head. You might want to gently relieve your neck of that poking-forwards-chicken thing, if you do what I do. I find it easier to do this on my side by making the pillow or pillows support my head so that, if you were looking at me from behind, there is no kink in my spine from right to left. There would be a straight line from the top of my head, down through my neck, down my spine, to my bum. Aim for the straight-line effect, while the pillows take the weight of your head.

On the other axis, that is forwards and backwards, you might want to experiment. Some nights, I go for the foetal curve. Other nights, I arch backwards. Whichever feels best and feels like it's relaxing your bones and muscles, go for it. One key thing. When you move, breathe out. Always breathe out on the move, whichever way you bend. This is a great relaxing mechanism. When you breathe out, imagine that you're breathing out through your back, in that space that's below your ribs and above your pelvis. You may well feel your body widening out down there and gently collapsing around and below your belly button on the front. If you concentrate on that feeling, that helps with relaxing too.

So there we have it.

To sum up:

- 'One good thing' principle.

- Lining up your spine and neck.

- Curving your spine gently forwards or backwards, breathing out on every move.

- Concentrating on the breathing (in with the nose, out through the mouth, counting the numbers for the length of in and out).

- Gentle (very gentle) stretching of any part of you that feels tight.

- The counting routine combined with the statue routine.

I cannot promise that this will work the first night that you try it. I cannot promise that it will always work for you every time.

All I can say is that it works for me, very nearly every time.

On occasion, I sleep four or five hours and wake up. It does sometimes happen that that's it, I haven't got any more sleep in me. So, rather than hang about in bed, making myself unhappy, I get up and have something to drink.

A couple of other things: I have completely stopped drinking alcohol and any drink with caffeine in it. This means that I pretty well only drink water, often hot water.

If I wake up at, say four or five, I put on an eye mask. I bought one online and it's brilliant. I make sure it's comfortable. I do my count-and-statue routine, and quite often I get another couple of hours' sleep.

That's it.

I hope it works.

Good nights make for good days.

As this whole section is a suggestion, I haven't got anything to add here, other than to say, 'Good night!'

O

is for On

(Pressing On, Pushing On, Getting On …)

When I was a kid, we followed a regular routine of having a big Sunday meal, usually at around one o'clock. We had this in the kitchen where the meal was cooked – usually by Mum, though my brother, our father and I did often help with peeling potatoes. In the kitchen in our first-floor flat, in winter, it was hot and steamy. There was a gas and coke fire near to the table where we sat; the window overlooking our backyard would steam up. We would often end up feeling woozy and slack.

At the end of the meal, there was a moment or two where the question of who would do the washing up would rise to the surface. As Mum had usually done the cooking, the real question was how my brother, our father and I would divvy it up. Our father had strong views on household chores: they should be shared. As far as my brother and I were concerned, I think he thought that was a good training. As I mentioned in E is for Experiment, he would urge us on with a shout of 'All for the collective!' He was very political.

It just so happens, that it didn't quite pan out as being 'all'. In that moment where the question came up of who would do the washing up, my brother and I noticed that our father would often push his chair back, push his hair back off his forehead with a tired stroke, give out a little grunt and say, 'Must press on, Con.' (Mum's name was Connie.)

He would then get up, sigh, walk slowly out of the kitchen, down the passage to the 'front room' where, as far as we knew, he would 'press on'. We didn't know what he was pressing on with, and we didn't know why he was pressing on with whatever he was pressing on with.

What we did know is that when he did this, it meant that we had to do the washing up. All for the collective.

It became such a familiar routine that my brother adopted it. If he was going out with his mates, he would get up from the table, push his hair back, do the little grunt and say to me, 'Must press on, Con,' and disappear out of the room. If he was busying about in the bedroom with one of his models, he would look up at me and say, 'Must press on, Con.'

Bit by bit, over the years, we got some inkling of what our father was pressing on with: there was the marking of schoolbooks when he was a classroom teacher. Then later there were 'talks' that he was going to give and articles he was going to write. For a few years, there was a PhD that he was writing. Interspersed amongst these were bursts of DIY: hanging wallpaper, painting skirting boards and a several weeks-long project of getting an old piano down the stairs. To cover all these, there was: 'Must press on, Con.'

There were times, though, that if you got near enough to see, you could make out that he wasn't doing any of these things. He was in fact reading an old copy of the *TV Times*, a magazine that he claimed to hate. One time, in May, my brother spotted he was reading a *TV Times* from November. What my brother had cracked with this investigation was that any bit of print on paper could serve as 'pressing on'. Words on a page were like magnets. He collected them, too. Every now and then he would run his fingers along a shelf and pull out a book that to my eyes was meaningless. One of them fitted into the palm of his hand. It had no pictures on its cover. There was no title on the cover either and it seemed to be made of some kind of plastic, but given that it was very, very, very old (he said), it couldn't have been plastic. When he opened it, I could see that it wasn't even in English. 'That's Latin, Mick,' he said. He pointed at where the book came from: Amsterdam. *People in Amsterdam must speak Latin*, I thought. '1624, Mick,' he said. Why would he want an Amsterdam Latin book from 1624? '*Utopia*,' he said. 'Thomas More's *Utopia*.' Then he flicked through a few pages and put it back on the shelf.

Much more interesting was to hear that he had bought it for a penny or two off a stall on Farringdon Road but really it was worth much more.

Clever father, I thought. That's what comes from 'pressing on, Con'. You press on, and then one day, you might be on Farringdon Road, see an old book, buy it for a penny but really it would be worth a fortune.

Sometimes, he would become concerned that either my brother or I were not pressing on. In my case, it could be a matter of 'playing out' with my friends. In my brother's case, it could be a matter of making model cars, model trains, model aeroplanes, model houses, model trees, and model people to put with the model cars, model trains, model aeroplanes, model houses and model trees, and then making lists of the model cars, model trains, model aeroplanes, model houses and model trees but also lists of real-life cars, trains, aeroplanes, houses and trees.

Our father didn't think that any of this was pressing on.

Even so, one way or another, via several diversions and excursions, my brother and I did press on. He pressed on with fossils. I pressed on with books. At some point, I got it that pressing on had something to do with something else: pressing on was related to getting on. I can put my finger on one key moment in this journey of discovery. There was a party. At the end of the party I got into a car. In the car was one person who, as it happens, did indeed get on hugely. She became one of this country's most famous interviewers. She was with a jokey, witty sort of guy with black hair. The moment we got into the car, he said, 'Rosen! You're getting on, aren't you? Are you getting on? Yes, I think you are getting on.' (You can see, he answered his own questions.)

I didn't think of myself as getting on. I thought of myself as 'doing stuff'.

And that's the point.

You see, I really do know the virtues of doing nothing. I know the virtues of doing very little. I'm not someone who thinks that doing nothing is evil and doing a lot is virtuous. I don't have in mind that the devil will find mischief for you to do if you're doing nothing. I'm not someone who thinks that God will love you if you do a lot. I do know that these ideas (or remnants of them) are very deeply ingrained in many of us in Western cultures no matter what our beliefs are. They're ingrained in me. All the more reason then for me to try to disentangle from the grip of these ideas, what there is that's helpful and hopeful.

I have an intuitive, unresearched, unevidenced feeling that there are people who are less happy than they could be because they can't find something to 'press on' with. I realise that this is a huge claim and it's easy to find objections to it. Like I said, it's intuitive. It's a hunch. And I don't want to infect it with Puritan notions of devils and a God with a frown on His face. Knowing how to do nothing is an art in itself that has to be worked at as hard as knowing what to do. It's a bit hypocritical, though, to write about doing nothing because it takes a lot of doing to write about doing nothing.

So how do we find what to do? How do we find something that is enjoyable and fulfilling? One thing we have to sort out is whether the stuff we're doing is really because we're trying to please the people who brought us up, and not because it's satisfying for ourselves. There's obviously no harm in pleasing your parents – quite the opposite; it's great to have their affirmation. One problem, though: if the only reason why we're doing something is to please them, then there's every chance it'll be a bottomless pit. Ultimately, it may never be enough. We'll always want more and more affirmation, or, tragically, there's only a little affirmation on offer and it never grows into more. Again, 'ultimately', you have to be satisfied with you. You have to satisfy you.

As I say, there's every reason to want and hope for affirmation for your parents but if we want to escape from the bottomless pit, it may be that we have to find affirmation from 'out there' and 'in here'.

I observe that some people really do find it 'in here'. I see them in garden centres and choirs. They're people who can get to feel calm and good through doing something that pleases them. They seem not to need the acclaim of hundreds, thousands or millions of others. They aren't as needy or as downcast as many of the rest of us are. In all honesty, I can't say that I am such a person. I have to confess that I am somebody who enjoys the affirmation of others and have been unbelievably lucky in getting a good deal of it. I realise that in saying that and in going into this territory of 'pressing on', I am coming from that hugely advantageous position. Even so, I'm staking the claim that 'doing stuff' is a route to having good days. Whether it's my father's version – pressing on – or some other kind of doing, is for each of us to figure out. I should say that as far as my father was concerned, he had to overcome poverty and tragedy before I knew him (that is, before I was born) and again when Mum died. I'm pretty sure that his version of doing stuff really did help him.

As I've written before, doing stuff was a huge help to me when my son died. The very fact that I had things to concentrate on, things that people wanted me to do, make and finish, was enormously beneficial. It meant that for several hours in a day, I wasn't in the pit of despair. I was in and around other people who wanted and needed something from me. I could concentrate on getting these things right, doing them well, listening to what other people wanted to say, representing their ideas through my work. As we say, 'it took me out of myself'. Good expression!

I'm also in the fortunate position of getting up every morning knowing that there's stuff for me to do. And even more fortunately, it's stuff that's enjoyable. When I get to the end of it, if other people are happy with it, then I feel good. Sometimes, I feel good before I hear what other people think of it. That's hard. Maybe it's hard for my kind of person, or maybe it's hard for most people. How do you reward yourself, how do you pat yourself on the back, how do you look in the mirror and say, 'Well done'? I'm still learning how to do that!

I think I get to that point when I can say to myself, 'I got it as right as ever I'll get something right.' So in that way, there has to be some acceptance by me. In my line of work, it may be because I found the right word, or the right pattern of words, or that I made things match, or that I matched words to sounds to feelings to thoughts to ideas in a way that 'clicked', in a way that works.

This means accepting that nothing is ever perfect *but* that's no reason to be dissatisfied. I know people who take the first part of that sentence in completely the other way: because nothing is ever perfect, you can never be satisfied. That seems to me to be a great shame. People much wiser and more knowledgeable than me will know how to help people get out of that knot. All I can say is that, yes, the world is imperfect, we are imperfect, what we do is imperfect but at some point, if you want to survive, we have to find ways to not let that feeling grind us down. Trying to do small things well and often might be one way out of the hole. In other words, pressing on, as my father said!

SUGGESTION

Draw up a list of all the things you do which come under the heading of 'getting on' (in a CV sense of the words).

Draw up another list of all the things that are necessary but not actually 'getting on' (housework, shopping, booking trips, etc.).

Draw up one more list of all the things that are just fun or relaxing or good ways to do nothing.

When you look at these three lists, ask yourself whether you have got the balance right.

P

is for Play

I often copy and paste documents from one source into something I'm typing. So I might copy something from a Facebook post across to an article I'm writing. As I'm on a Mac, the files I'm typing are on a system called 'Pages'. This means that I might sometimes want to copy across to Pages from a Microsoft file.

I've been doing this sort of thing for as long as I've been on computers.

Suddenly, one day, when I tried to do this simple and very useful procedure, the copied text that appeared on my 'Pages' page was a set of question marks. No words. Just question marks in boxes. At first, I thought that I had lost the text I had copied. Of course, that made me cross. I started poking keys on my keyboard but all that happened is that some of the question marks disappeared. I was cross because I thought that I would have to end up typing out large sections of text. I muttered, 'Waste of bloody time,' to myself.

I started to prepare one of my anti-technology speeches in my head in which I was going to rave on to someone nearby how at the very moment technology makes things easy, it puts obstacles in our way. I conjured up images of people like Jesse Eisenberg playing Mark Zuckerberg in the movie *Social Network* sitting about in unlit rooms in California, thinking up new, nerdy 'facilities', 'shortcuts' and 'cheats' in order to make billions. I imagined that this question mark thing was just a way for someone to cream off a tax as I moved from one operating system to another. 'Gor! It's just like the bloomin' toll gates on turnpike roads in the eighteenth century …!' (Even when I'm angry, you can see I can get quite graphic with my imagery.)

But then something clicked in, something that held me back from busting a blood vessel over this: the play reflex. What is this? The play reflex says in a circumstance like this: don't fret, don't rant. Just fiddle.

And what is fiddling?

Fiddling in this case means using my eyes, fingers and brain to see what might happen if. That's it. What might happen if. After all, this wasn't a life-or-death moment. Nothing huge was at stake. A few moments of my work-time perhaps, but let's not get too self-important about that. I was just writing a talk about a story.

My brain knows stuff about the internet. I've been on it since about 1997. I know stuff about word processing. I have written hundreds of thousands of words on computers. I can do some but not all 'formatting'. That's my 'knowledge base'.

I can touch-type. That's my 'skills base'.

With all that I can, if I want to, go into databases, bibliographies and search engines to find 'What to do' and 'Can we help?' pages. Confession: I find these helpful but only up to a point. That's because I don't have two screens, so in order to follow their flow charts and procedures, I have to print out what they say and have it by my side as I follow it. Something in me resists this. I don't know why. So let's just park that.

Instead, what I do is start roaming about my computer's text-processing systems, while casually seeking out internet pages. It feels to me as if there must be kinds of spark or synapses in my brain firing off, throwing up messages like, 'Why don't you try such-and-such?' 'Why don't you try so-and-so?'

Having tried various routes and reached dead ends, another spark flashed up saying, 'Why don't you go to the menu that runs alongside your page of text which is now covered in question marks in boxes?'

I now know from previous free-ranging excursions on my word-processing pages, that in that menu is a clear box which, if I pull down the arrow on the side, it gives me a set of options which I have experimented with, like 'Label Dark', 'Heading Red' and 'CAPTION' – rather poetic in their own way, don't you think? I could make a little performance poem-chant out of that.

Anyway, I've found on this menu one of the most useful suggestions, the one that is mysteriously called 'Body'. (Add that to the poem-chant.) I've discovered through my experiments in the past that if ever I've wanted to get rid of unwanted font changes or line breaks and the like, I can 'select all', hit 'Body' and the whole text becomes one unified format, clean of these unwanted differences. For some mysterious reason it also shrinks the text down to near-invisible size but that's easily remedied by increasing the size.

What if, I wondered, I 'select all' of the question marks in boxes and hit 'Body'? Nothing to lose. If it doesn't work, I can always go back, copy the text that I copied before, and try another route. So I did it. 'Select all', and 'Body'. Booooom! The question marks in boxes disappeared and the copied text appeared.

It worked!

From this point on, I now had a procedure that I could use whenever these question marks in boxes have appeared. Go to 'Body'. In other words, I not only know how to do something, I have learned it off by heart.

This tells me that on this occasion, play works. I have used the knowledge I have (k.i.h.) to help me get the knowledge I need (k.i.n.). To get me from k.i.h. to k.i.n. I've used play.

No one instructed me. I didn't even use an instruction manual. I just fiddled.

This is one kind of play. I'm going to describe it as 'trial and error without fear of failure'. I'm also going to make huge claims for it. That is: that through play we investigate and discover how the world works, how it could or might work in the future. Most of us do this on a small scale almost every day. Some of us do a lot of it every day. Some of the world's greatest and most important discoveries and inventions have had at least one stage in their evolution which involved 'trial and error without fear of failure'.

Not all scientists, technologists, artists, mathematicians, architects and inventors are open and frank about the kind of play they used to get from k.i.h to k.i.n. And even when they are, for some reason to do with how we view knowledge, we often relegate these moments or hide them behind talk of 'genius', 'breakthroughs', 'eureka moments' and the like. And yet, it's difficult to see how any step change in what the human race knows, has been achieved without play. One simple reason for that: if we restrict ourselves to operating with what we know, and never experiment in order to find out or invent something new, we will only stay with what we know. Or, put another way, what we know will always be a necessary condition for discovery and invention but not a sufficient one. We need to be in that space of mind in which we can try and fail without fear of failure to take us to the next stage.

My next big claim is to say that playing makes us happy. When we play, we have a good time. A good day, in fact. After I had made my big discovery of how to get rid of a page full of question marks in boxes, my irritation evaporated. I had an immediate sense of achievement (no, really, I'm not kidding), I congratulated myself (self-esteem went through the roof), and I felt good. This was my 'one good thing' that I could carry over to the just-before-sleep routine that I've described in N is for Nights.

In case you're feeling cynical about all this and you're thinking that I've told this story as some kind of ego trip to boost my flagging morale, let me tell you about Alessandro Volta. You know about him even if you don't know about him. Well, you would, if you've ever said, written or read the word 'volt'. Volts are named after Signor Volta. If you don't already know, I can tell you that this is because Volta did something big in the field of electricity.

Our world relies on electricity. The world before Volta didn't rely on electricity. The world before Volta had figured that there was some kind of energy around but that it seemed to be in animals. One scientist (Galvani) thought that there was some kind of 'animal electric fluid'.

Volta had other ideas.

(If you are squeamish about frogs, look away now.)

Galvani thought frogs' legs contained this fluid and that it flowed into metal, which he attempted to prove by connecting metal wire to the nerves of a dead frog's leg to see if it twitched. Later, Volta got to work, experimenting (playing!) to find out which metals worked best. Silver and zinc seemed to be best.

Now here comes the big breakthrough. Volta put the silver and zinc in his mouth. And he felt a tingle. (Please don't try this at home.)

He reversed this. He connected the silver and zinc to wires and put the wires in his mouth. No tingle.

He figured that the silver and zinc had to be wet.

I'm now going to leave Signor Volta with his silver, zinc and saliva, other than to say that it was at this moment the human race discovered (or perhaps definitely confirmed) that under certain conditions, in certain circumstances, 'current' could flow through metal. And later, with the addition of jars of water and a lot else, Volta worked out how to make something like a battery.

I don't know if Alessandro Volta died a happy man. I am prepared to bet my boots, though, on my guess that the day he felt that first tingle was a good day.

As I said, that's one kind of play. There are many others. The most common is rule-based play, in games where we didn't make up the rules. Right from our first games with Ludo or 'catch' or beach cricket through to organised sport, many of us play games. I'm keen on plenty of them, good at very few of them. I like watching them. I can't get away from the fact that if you win, you feel great, but (big but) if you lose you don't feel so great. Or, you have to do a lot of work on yourself, to not feel at the very least slightly pissed off that you lost that game of table tennis, Monopoly or tiddlywinks. I speak as someone who has spent zillions of hours playing Scrabble, Monopoly, Shove Ha'penny, 'who had the last hit?', 'football-tennis', deck tennis, wrestling, pinball, mile-walking, rugby, 100-metre breaststroke swimming, fantasy football and on and on and on.

But I'm going to leave them where they can look after themselves. Often making us feel great. Sometimes landing us with feelings of inadequacy. That's fine. I know the argument about that: we can learn from those feelings too.

This P is for Play, though, is about this other kind of play. Some call it 'free play'. I've already called it 'experimenting' elsewhere in this book as well.

One aspect of it that I haven't made clear is that there is no limit to the medium you can play in or with. Think of the arts. Across the arts we see people using every material that humans have ever come across or invented – stone, wood, paint, paper, cardboard, plastic (and more). Artists have used their bodies, as when dancers dance. Music artists use banging, scraping, scratching, blowing on materials and objects or just using their own bodies. The world of literature uses the human invention of language, projected through the media of print or screens, performed using our bodies (voices and drama). You could go on with this list. In each and all of these arts, there will be moments of play for every practitioner who has ever been or ever will be. When we look at the ceiling of the Sistine Chapel, hear Miles Davis's *Kind of Blue*, watch Pina Bausch's dance or any art that we admire and love, it sometimes feels so perfect, so finished, that it's hard to see or imagine the wonderful moments of trial and error that the artist was immersed in on the way. Perhaps that's why play gets so neglected or even rejected in how we view ourselves or in how we bring up our children or indeed in how we run our lives as adults, deep in our problems of earning enough, being safe enough, being part of a group of people who care enough. Play can often seem frivolous, unnecessary or a waste of time.

I say, find your medium. Pastry, plants, your body, your voice, a musical instrument, clay, wood – anything … and make time to play with it.

And don't punish yourself with it. Remember always that it's trial and error without fear of failure that does the trick.

I'll finish with this: you may or may not know the book, *We're Going on a Bear Hunt*. It's an adaptation by me of many versions of a folk rhyme or folk song that appeared sometime in the 1950s in the 'Brownies' (from the Scouting movement) and from American children's summer camps. My version is incredibly, beautifully, wonderfully and creatively imagined by Helen Oxenbury. She created the strong imagery of the family so full of expectation, wonder and fear. When I meet children, we often perform the piece together. Every time I do it, I do it differently. I explain to the children that that's what we can do with rhymes and songs. They don't have to be exactly the same. Indeed, the great Irish singer Van Morrison says the same when he performs.

So when I do *Bear Hunt* with children I get them to join in with new sounds and actions so that that day, that moment will be unique. But also, so that they pick up the idea that they can make up new versions later, tomorrow, next week or whenever. Even so, we invariably come back to the book, and young children will often ask me about the picture of the bear on the last page of the book. In this picture, the bear (we nearly always assume it's the same bear as the one we met in the cave) is in the middle of a double-page spread of the sea at night. The bear is walking away from us, its feet in the wavelets that are breaking on the beach. The moon is high in the night sky, shining onto the sea and sand. If we think of the bear as having human feelings and doing human actions, then it rather looks as if the bear is fed up. It appears to be slightly hunched or slumped. It's clearly not running or jumping. If anything, we might imagine that it's dragging its feet in the water.

What do children ask me about the bear?

They say, 'What's the bear thinking?' or 'Why's the bear sad?'

What do I say?

I say, 'I don't know.'

What I really mean is 'I don't know any better or any more than you do', but it's a bit difficult to say that to very young children without sounding off-putting. So, actually what I say, all run together is:

'I-don't-know. What-do-you-think?'

And they tell me!

If there's a group of them, they play. They act out being the bear, they throw up all sorts of possibilities about what the bear's thinking: 'He's sad.' 'It wanted to be friends.' 'It's lonely.'

'It only wanted to play.'

They use evidence from the shape or look of the bear and remind themselves of what came before when the children seemed to have surprised the bear in its cave. 'It was only trying to sleep.' 'The bear's lonely.'

In this way, playing with possibilities, the children get to what they feel is a key part of the story. That's not just a matter of how the children feel. As it's a participation song, the 'we' of the story, means that it's 'us' who go on the bear hunt as well as the children 'in' the story. The picture also asks us to reverse that egocentric view of the story and gets us thinking and wondering how the bear feels about it. Through play (it's a form of 'dramatic play'), we experience and develop empathy: what would it feel like to be that bear in that situation, at that time, having experienced what that bear just experienced?

With my more teacherly hat on, I might take this play on to another shape. Sometimes, I say, 'Hey, let's make up a chorus for the bear … something like, "I'm a bear. I'm a bear." Then each of us think up something that the bear's thinking, and say it.'

So what happens is that we all say, 'I'm a bear. I'm a bear,' like a chant (or any other chorus we can invent) and each child can speak as if they're the bear, things like:

'I'm lonely.'

'I'm a bear. I'm a bear.'

'I only wanted to play.'

'I'm a bear. I'm a bear.'

'I'm going back to my cave.'

'I'm a bear. I'm a bear.'

And so on, till we've got what may be a 30-line chant.

Do you know where I got that idea from? From a field recording that the great US folklorist Alan Lomax made in a state penitentiary. He recorded a group of men on a chain gang singing a song made of lines and a chorus about 'a grizzly,

grizzly bear'. As we know from ethnographic studies, work-songs, shanties and many call-and-response songs all over the world involve improvisation and … play!

By the way, the 'grizzly bear' in the song that Lomax recorded is a coded or metaphorical way of talking about the overseer or guard. The men singing the song were all African American men. The overseer is white. The history of slavery was not far behind this scene. In the lines they sing in front of this man are hidden ideas about escaping from him or bringing him down.

That's yet another way in which we feed 'what we know' into 'how we play'.

You can find the recording if you search online!

SUGGESTION

Find time to play – trial and error without fear of failure. Something joyful, or silly or purposeless in any medium you like: food, clay, words, drawing, funny voices, textiles, music, dressing up, dance ... anything.

What happens if you break all the rules that you were taught in any of these fields? What happens if you improvise?

What happens if you break out of your 'knowledge-zone' and go into a medium you were told you were 'not good at', or you've always said to yourself you're no good at?

If you shut the door so you're on your own, no one can see you dance! That's a good principle to remember.

Q
is for Quest

Here's a poem I wrote after I came out of hospital in 2020.

Two physiotherapists come over and sit on the sofa.
They ask me
'What are your long-term objectives?' I think, have I got any of them?
I wonder: have I ever had long-term objectives? I don't think so.
'What are your long-term objectives, right now?' they say.
'To be able to walk to the end of the street,
     go to the Jewish deli and remember what I went there for.'
That would be good, I think.
'Yes,' they say.
'Anything else?'
'Live for a bit more?' I say,
'And, come to think of it,
I've never bothered to make pickled cucumbers, I just buy them
but my mother made lovely pickled cucumbers
I would like to try that one day.'

'You're doing very well,' they say.

I think this was the first time in my life anyone had ever asked me what my 'long-term objectives' were and it threw me. And, as you can see, I don't think I had ever really thought about it. I do meet people, though, who do have long-term objectives. One person, very kindly, said that his long-term objective was to be like me. I took it as a compliment, but you have to be careful about these things. It's possible he had noticed some-thing really revolting about me and it was this that he wanted to be like. You can't tell, can you? (Irony alert)

Anyway, once I fixed on what the physiotherapists were talking about, you can see that I had some plans in my mind all the time: get to the Jewish deli, remember what I went there for, to live, and to make pickled cucumbers. I'm not sure whether that's in order of importance though.

At that moment, at that time, these were all good and reason-able objectives. In fact, these were, in their own way, quests. To tell the truth, there's a part of me that curls my lip the moment I say that. With my kind of background, quests are noble, fictional, fantastical, fabulous things: Odysseus plunging over the waves trying to get home; Sir Gawain trying to find the Green Knight; Dorothy, the Lion, the Scarecrow and the Tin Man trying to find the wizard or even Holden Caulfield in *The Catcher in the Rye* trying to find himself. (Did he? I'm not sure.)

These are overarching quests but in most stories even the small characters, the ordinary people, the walk-ons and the extras have their own 'story-arc'. That's to say, nearly every-one in any play, film or novel has a purpose and motive and pursues it, even if it's only, say, someone delivering a message. Their quest is to deliver the message. I mention delivering a message because, once, I played that messenger. Yes, I had that massive part that you will of course remember: the guy who comes on in *Romeo and Juliet* looking for someone who can help him. This is how it goes: I have an invite in my hand but I can't read it, so I say to myself: 'I am sent to find those persons whose names are here writ, and can never find what names the writing person hath here writ. I must to the learned.'

In one stroke, Shakespeare gives this tiny character a quest to perform. Luckily, it turns out that I don't have to go far because there's a person nearby who can read – Romeo.

The irony here, though, is that the paper I can't read is an invite to come to a ball at the house of the Capulets. On the list is the name of Romeo's love interest, Rosaline. Good, but Romeo (spoiler alert) is a member of the enemy Montague family. (Remember? The 'ancient feud'!) So it is that my quest ends up setting in motion the cogs that will lead to the highs and tragic lows of what's to come: Romeo vows to ignore the feud between the two families and go to the ball anyway. That's Romeo's immediate quest, embedded as it is in his over-all quest for love. Quests can be embedded in other quests.

In passing, I should say that my quest (as an actor) should have been to concentrate on who I am and what I'm trying to do. In other words, to focus on the quest to find someone to read my message and, given who I am (a servant), how I'm going to handle that quest, or any setbacks or any help I may get along the way. If I had been a good actor, I could have established for myself what kind of well-meaning, obedient guy I am. I could have asked myself questions about whether I thought 'my master' treats me well, and also how I comport myself in these dangerous streets where people get stabbed to death just for being part of the 'wrong' family or in that family's entourage. But I'm not a good actor so instead, I bumbled onto the stage trying to get a laugh. In other words, my own personal quest was so different from the character's quest that I distracted from the scene. Bad. Really bad bit of work. Shameful.

I should have been attentive to my acting quest but not in such a way that it clashed with the overall objective of the other actors; the other characters' quests; and the point of the play at that moment. I sit here now wishing that the direc-tor had taken me to one side and told me to stop mucking about and concentrate on what it must have been like for someone (a servant) who couldn't read. There! That simple. The matter in hand.

I take from all this several things. All day, every day, most of us have small quests.

Practical hint: if you don't already do it, start every day with a 'To Do' list. These are, of course, quests. (One problem with mine. If I do my 'To Do' list last thing at night and leave it on the table, one of our cats brings it upstairs to the bedroom at four in the morning and leaves it by the side of the bed. What?! What do the cats know? What are they telling me?)

Some of us also have big overarching quests. If we pursue these quests in ways that screw up other people, then maybe we've got something wrong. Of course, what with everyone else pursuing their own quests, there are bound to be clashes.

By the by, two literary points: if you're in any way interested in writing or in any way interested in analysing a novel, play or film, it's worth asking yourself questions about overarching and small-scale quests: what does the character want? What or who is getting in the way of that? What or who is helping them? There's a follow-up question, too. By the end of the scene or the story, did the person fulfil their quest? Did they get what they wanted? You'll remember from the King Arthur story that the overarching quest is to find the Holy Grail. They all try but only one knight gets it. (It just so happens he's the most boring of all the knights, but don't tell anyone, it'll spoil the story.)

So, let me stick with this idea that all day, every day, we have small quests, like make a cup of tea, get to the bus stop on time, pay the overdue bill, buy the milk, bread and fruit – that sort of thing. At the same time, arching over the top of them, we might have big quests, like have children, or move to Ireland, or be happy, or find myself. Now, I said that when we get to the end of stories (whether we've written them, or read or watched them) we can ask, did the character get what they were looking for? Did they achieve what they set out to achieve? In tragedies, like *Othello* or *Hamlet*, let's say, it's often a yes and a no, at the same time: the main character realises how everything worked (that's the yes) while at the very same moment this character's world has fallen apart (that's the no).

But hang on, should we set ourselves quests anyway?

My idea of 'one good thing' (see N is for Nights) implies that I'm looking to do one good thing, so that I can concentrate on it and give myself approval for it. That said, there is an approach that says, I don't always have to look for the good thing. An opportunity or occasion will arise, merely by being in the world, for me to do something that is 'good enough': like scratching that itch I've got on the side of my nose. It could end up being a really good scratch. Remember it. Hoard it. Retell it to myself later. Good enough.

Clearly, the physios in my first story thought that I ought to have an overarching quest. I guess that they work with people who've sunk into melancholy and depression following major illnesses and accidents. I guess further that they think that it helps people in that situation to think ahead to next year, or even to the next ten years, because thinking like that gives you a rope that you can throw ahead of yourself, sling it onto to a hook and haul yourself towards it.

That makes sense.

I will admit, though, that until the physios said that, I hadn't ever really thought about it. I know why. It's because I'm one of those ludicrously fortunate people who (as I've tried to explain elsewhere in the book) is either being given or is setting himself stuff to do, projects, objectives, quests! If I were to be ruthlessly honest about myself (never a very comfortable thing to do), when the physios asked me those questions, I had several 'ropes' that I was hauling myself along anyway: radio programmes to make, Zoom calls to schools to prepare for, books to write, family life to be part of, my wife Emma and I to look after each other, help each other …

What if you don't have the 'ropes'? What if you can't find them? Or make them happen? What if there seems to be no point? Does it help for someone like my physios to say to you, 'So? What are your long-term objectives?' (I have a realisation here that I've turned them into characters a bit like the witches in *Macbeth*, though instead of telling me my destiny – as the witches tell Macbeth – they are telling me to make my own destiny.) Does it help you to at least make yourself aware that you could think of long-term objectives? Perhaps we do need people to do that to us every now and then so that's why I'm doing it here.

Not that it's comfortable. Think of those moments at some slightly posh do, when you're standing there awkwardly gobbling canapés and someone comes up to you, puts their head on one side and says to you, 'And what do YOU doooo?' Or, think back to those careers chats at school or college when the person on the other side of the table stares at you and says, 'What would you really *like* to do?'

What's really uncomfortable about that is that our TV screens are full of massively successful people who bubble with joy as they tell us about how they've pursued their dreams, they've done what they really wanted to do, it's all worked out and … (here comes the fib) … we can all do it! (Can we? No, we can't all play for Real Madrid, break a world record, or sing a chartbusting hit. So please don't say that!)

What we can do is have realistic quests. I know that sounds deadly dull, but I have said to young people many times that that is all I've ever done – not that I'm a great model for everything! In short, I go for the realistic day-by-day quests. The To-Do list. The overarching one may emerge. Or it may not. What really matters (I think) is not so much the big dream (big quest) as much as the state of mind I'm in from day to day while I do the small stuff.

Put another way, anyone can set themselves big quests. As I've said, they're being dangled in front of us on TV every day. There are hundreds of hugely successful, glittery, glamorous, clever people being shown to us. Any of us can *say* to ourselves, 'I want to be like her. I want to be like him.' What's much harder is to set ourselves a realistic task to fulfil a realisable quest today or tomorrow. When one of these works out, it hits the button. And every time it works out in my life, I've actually learned something. Each bit of learning builds on the last bit of learning. Each bit of learning paves the way for the next bit of learning.

That's the bit about fulfilling the objective, the bit that's analogous to the question we ask of characters in stories: did she get what she wanted? We say that Cinderella did. King Lear didn't. What about ourselves? Can we, dare we, ask of ourselves: did I fulfil my overarching quest? I think it's reasonable and hugely comforting to say of the small quests that we did. I think that even trying to say of the overarching quest (if you have one) 'I fulfilled it', is a risky business. But then I know of myself, I would say that, because I'm quite risk-averse. You could almost say that being risk-averse is one of my quests: 'I will do this next thing in a risk-averse way.'

I hope it helps you for me to say that.

Meanwhile, I'm still thinking about my physiotherapists. What I should have said was that there are some long-term objectives (quests) that I only know about after I've done them. My life is littered with failed quests. I have tried many, many times to get projects off the ground that have looked promising and then nosedived into the bin: ideas for books, radio programmes, TV programmes, articles, jobs I could apply for. I've got filing cabinets full of them. (That dates me!) Just as often, people have approached me with a project, told me how great it's going to be and would I spend some time working on it to get it going? I carry memories of them in my mind, sitting on my sofa, waving their arms about. Or I see them in their offices, on the fifth floor of glass and silver towers. And such enthusiasm! So I do the work, but then everything goes quiet and I never hear from the person again. Really. Nothing. Zilch. Not even a 'sorry but this project won't be going ahead'. Maybe they forget how to write.

Every time either of these two routes to potential projects arise, I'm full of hope that they'll happen. (A day of hope is a good day to have, I find. Hope is good.) Then when the projects collapse, I have to bring in Teflon-plated armour to make sure I'm not fed up about it. Say, 'tomorrow is a new day'. Say, 'it wouldn't have worked anyway'. In fact, the best remedy here is to carry on with the quests I was running anyway, the ones where it's down to me to finish, where my destiny was in my own hands in the first place.

Then, when I look back over these finished quests, something emerges. I can see that a stream of small quests represents an overall pattern, or intention even. They show me myself, consistently heading in the same direction. The small quests are like bricks in the arch of an overarching quest. It's just that I wasn't aware of it at the time.

So, physiotherapists, I should have said something like this to you. I should have said, 'I don't know what the long-term objective is at the moment, but I'll know what it is after I've done the small stuff. That'll be at the end of a "long term", as it were.'

Somewhere in there is a joke about having an objective that comes after the event and not before it. It's a nonsense, but I know what I mean!

SUGGESTION

The basic one is in this section – make your own lists.

Then there's the mother of all lists, the list of lists: explore the possibility that life is a list!

R

is for Reflection

I'm sitting in a class on motor nerves. The teacher, a kindly bearded man, is drawing with chalk on a blackboard. (Actually, it's green, but that's not important in this bit of the story.) He writes the letter 'S'. He draws a horizontal line from the 'S' and puts an arrowhead on the end of it. He then draws the letter 'R' next to the arrowhead. He then says, 'Stimulus → Response.'

He asks us to chop each other's knees just below our knee-caps. We do and we observe our legs involuntarily jerking upwards. He talks of hot water being dropped onto our hands and how we would quickly pull our hands away. He talks about the 'motor reflex'.

My friend Robert, who is keen on disrupting thought and mind, because (I think) he spent three years at the Sorbonne studying philosophy, asks me later whether I think all thought is S → R. I think for a moment. Why not? Someone says something; we react. It's S → R, I say. Robert's eyes twinkle behind his French glasses. On the paper in front of him is the S → R diagram:

$$S \rightarrow R$$
$$\text{Stimulus} \rightarrow \text{Response}$$

He then draws a vertical line down through the arrow, crossing it. He labels it 'C'. I have no idea what this is or why he's doing it. He explains. It's true that there are motor responses like your knee reflex, he says, but that doesn't explain all action, surely. Why not? I say. Because of 'C', he says. What's 'C'? I say.

'Aha,' he says. 'How significant that you don't know.' This is irritating but also enjoyable.

'Can you guess?' he says.

'Capability?' I say.

'Nope,' he says, 'it's consciousness.'

This is all sounding much too abstract for me to get my head round.

He explains: 'Yes, we are bombarded with stimuli but before we respond, the stimuli land up in our minds, in our consciousness. We process the stimuli and then respond.'

'Right,' I say. 'I'll think about that.'

'Exactly,' he says with a twinkle.

When I think about it, I experiment. I jam a piece of bread that is too thick into the toaster. I go out the room. It's too thick to pop up. The toast burns. Someone says to me, 'Fool!' I react: 'No, I'm not.'

Is that S → R? Or is it S → C → R?

Hmm. Maybe Robert is right, I think. After all, I might say, 'No I'm not,' but someone else might say, 'Sorry, how daft of me.'

We each have the same stimulus but we react to that stimulus differently because of C, because of who we are, because of how our different minds have developed, because of our consciousness.

Next time I see Robert, I tell him of my brilliant example of the toaster.

He says, 'Yep, we're reflective creatures. Outside of motor reflexes, we reflect on the stimuli we're given and our response is a result of how we reflected on the stimulus.'

That's that then. Sorted. We are reflective creatures. We go about reflecting on what's thrown at us, and acting accordingly. I like that. But then he gets out a bit of paper. He draws S → C → R. He now draws another arrow. This runs from

R (response), back towards S (stimulus). He looks at me. I look at the drawing. *How can R do something to S?* I think.

'The response affects the stimulus,' he says.

'Oh, does it?' I say.

'You sound dismayed,' he says.

'It's just that you're complicating it,' I say.

'Yep,' he says, 'but think about it. We're talking to each other. We're bombarding each other with stimuli. Our consciousnesses are reflecting on the stimuli and we're responding to each other. But what's also going on is that when you respond to me, that affects me. I change. Next time I give out a stimulus, it's been affected by how you responded.'

I stare at the paper. Before I take it all in, he's added another S above the first S but this time it's squiggly. It's been changed by the response, I suppose. And then off goes an arrow from the squiggly S towards the R which has also got a new R next to it, because it too changed. And running downwards through all the arrows is the C arrow, consciousness.

He then adds on the bottom 'ad infinitum'.

'We're constantly giving each other stimuli, reflecting on them, responding, changing, responding, changing, responding and on and on and on. We are in fact not just reflecting creatures. We are reflecting, reflexive creatures.'

'And in your model,' I say, 'when the responder responds, doesn't that response become the stimulus to the person who delivered the first stimulus? Shouldn't the R (response) be an S (stimulus) on the second time round, going back?'

'Yes,' Robert says.

To cut this story off at this point, I can say, hand on heart, that I've never been the same since. Leaving aside those motor reactions, I see we humans relating to each other, in our thoughts and actions, embedded in these reflective–reflexive processes. We are not automatons and machines that simply leap into action or blurt things out because someone has pressed a 'Go!' button. The insult word for that is 'mechanistic'. Instead, we can say that in human interaction, there is always a 'C' (consciousness) that works on the 'S' (stimulus). There is always a way in which the 'R' (response) becomes an 'S' (stimulus) which arcs back to the original 'S' (stimulus) person which reflexively affects the 'S' (stimulus) person, via that person's 'C' (consciousness).

And what's this got to do with having a good day? Quite a lot actually!

We all 'mull stuff over'; we muse, ponder, wonder, consider and, indeed, reflect. I think we need time to do this every day. It probably needs time away from TVs, computers, phones and other people, when the only thing you're listening to is your thoughts. When I do this, I find that the key coordinates of the real world – like space and time – disappear. When I'm in my thoughts, memories become the present or mix with ideas about the future, all in a split second. Since I came out of hospital, I've started to have what I can only call hypersensory flashes. I'm in the midst of doing something ordinary, like spreading hummus on a bagel, and I'll get a flash of someone's face or a flash of someone's clothes from just recently, or from 70 years ago. And this isn't just a vague, cloudy memory. It's something really sharp, acute and detailed. One example: I had a friend at school called James. We invented a mocking laugh sound, which I'll represent here as 'Heeeaaa!' While I was spreading the hummus, James's face from 70 years ago came right into my mind, along with the exact way he held his mouth, how his eyes looked and – this is the bit that spooks me – the exact colour, shape and texture of his jacket, and the way that it fitted him. It all came to me uncalled for, as it were, in a flash. What's more, I can now summon up that image, whenever I want.

This feels quite strange to me. Even stranger is that this happens with images of many, many of my friends, relations, places and rooms from those times – that is, anytime up until I was about 30. For some reason, perhaps to do with the strange illness I had for many years – extreme hypothyroidism – the images that come to me from after that are less intense, less detailed.

It feels overall that I have some kind of strange power. I can either choose to bring up people, places and moments, or they will pop up anyway, and for a brief moment, I 'live' that moment. I'm in it. Quite often, I'll write about it – which I'll talk about in W is for Writing.

So this is one kind of reflection. If I speak for it, advocating it, I can say – to use a bit of jargon – it makes me feel 'connected'. To tell the truth, when I talk to people who tell me that there are vast chunks – many years even – of their childhoods that they can't 'find', can't recollect, I'm mystified. I wonder for a moment how it is they can live in the world! I go on to wonder, how can any of us live in the world if we don't know where we come from? Of course, they do know where they come from, but they don't need or don't want that intense, detailed connection with these bits of the past.

I also wonder if I've taught myself how to do this. Have the years of trying to write about these moments – I'll call them the 'roots of consciousness', if I may – stirred up memories that for some people stay dormant? One joy I have is meeting up with old school friends or sharing stuff with them by email or social media in which we home in on shared moments like our PE teacher yelling at us on cross-country runs in his strong central European accent: 'LIFT UP ZOSE GREAT FLET FEET, LADDY!' I can see his car, see the megaphone he is shouting through. I can see the shorts I'm wearing, the trees I'm running past. I can even see the PE kit and faces of some of the other kids.

This leads me to meaning. Yes, the meaning of life, if you like.

I know talking about this gets a bad press. We're really not supposed to admit to wondering, thinking or talking about such a thing. To talk about the meaning of life is a bit like farting in public. Even so, here it comes – and with some reflection.

I have grown up and I live without any reference to any deity, or outside force. Some people express that as 'I don't believe in God' or some such, but that's only a negative. The point is not what I 'believe' but how I live. That's to say, I live without a god or anything supernatural. I just refer to other human beings and the material state of the world. That feels to me like enough.

This means that I don't think there's any afterlife, or indeed any purpose to what we do here. So what we need to do (I think) is make the best of it while we're here. That's my reflection on the matter. But there's more. If there's no purpose, then ultimately, it's absurd. Back to the S–C–R: it goes like this: when I see a glass of water on the table, I have a thought about drinking water. I reach over to the glass; I lift it and pour it into my mouth. It's lovely. My knowledge also tells me that that water is going to go through my body doing all sorts of useful stuff like washing out the waste products of my metabolism that would be dangerous to me if they hung about in my body too long. The whole activity of seeing, lifting, drinking is full of purpose. It's not absurd. In fact, doing it is part of how today is good. I drink loads of water. (Some days I forget to drink loads of water and that's a bad day.)

But life, in contrast to me drinking the water, has no end beyond itself (I think). So, it's absurd. In fact, there are ways in which it's funny, as the absurd often is. And I find that to think of life as funnily absurd is comforting.

Let's start small. Every morning, I take pills. I have to push the pills out of their little homes on a strip of silver foil. It's easy but tricky. As I do it, there's every chance that I'll push it too hard, or too carelessly so that the pill pops out onto the floor, or into the sink. If it pops onto the floor, I then have to go looking for it. The floor is tiled in black and white. The pills are white. There's every chance that I won't find the pill. I go down on all fours, making sweeping movements with my hand. I worry about the cats and think that, if I don't find it, they'll come in, smell a tasty pill (why do I think a cat will think it's tasty? I dunno) eat it and die (why will they die from one pill of levothyroxine? I dunno, but it's what I think). So I'm kneeling on the bathroom floor making sweeping movements, hunting for a tiny pill.

I confess. This sort of thing used to make me ratty. I would make cursing noises, muttering 'fukettyfuketty' things under my breath. And I have a really irritating thing I do, which is pull back my lips, tutting and shaking my head. I say 'irritating' because it irritates other people and it also irritates me that I do this irritating thing. No. Used to do.

You see, now that I've 'reflected' on the absurd, on the non-meaning of life, I can see that this thing I'm doing, kneeling on the floor making sweeping movements, is absurd. In the great run of things, it really doesn't matter. It's just another tiny, tiny, tiny, tiny, tiny blip-moment in the history of the universe.

So, is this about proportion? I think so. Because surely I can't think that everything that's happened to me or that I do is absurd? The key thing here is not only proportion, but also what that phrase, 'making the best of it', means. What it means to my mind, on reflection, is that if life is pointless, we have to fight to make sure that it's not valueless in the here and now. This means that dropping my pill is both proportionally tiny but is also nigh-on valueless. It won't kill the cat. I've got plenty more pills. The only reason why I got irritated about it in the past was because it reminded me of my own looming incapacity. Well, sod that. Looming incapacity is reality, man. Just another bit of the absurd. Shakespeare again. Seven ages of man. '*Sans* teeth, *sans* eyes' and all that ('*sans*' meaning 'without'). Yes, he grasped the absurdity there, didn't he?

But while I'm talking about 'proportion', what should I make of the big stuff that's happened to me? Is the death of Eddie, my son, absurd? And if I say that it is, does that help me?

In a way, yes.

This is how I figure it. To start off with, after Eddie died, I couldn't get away from the idea that in some way or another, this was a punishment. At first, I thought that Eddie was punishing me. I'm ashamed of that. It was a terrible thought to have. It was blaming the victim and making his illness about me, as if somehow or another he got ill deliberately to do something to me. Awful thing to think.

Then, when I got rid of that thought, I moved the punishment out into the universe. Eddie dying was the universe punishing me. Remember, I don't refer to a god, so I couldn't say to myself it was God or a god punishing me or in fact doing anything at all – like teaching me a lesson, or helping me realise the importance of love or some such. So I have Eddie, me and the universe.

Then I thought some more. Everything I know about the universe is that it too has no purpose, no consciousness, no values. It can neither punish me nor reward me. What we call 'luck' or 'chance' are just intuitive comments about maths and statistics. They're not really about thoughts, feelings and values – the stuff we say that matters. So, no, Eddie dying had nothing to do with the universe talking to me.

This just leaves physiology – how our bodies work. Viruses, bacteria, antigens, antibodies, cells, blood, heart, membranes and the like.

But Robert drew that line down through the arrow between S and R. The C arrow. I've got C for consciousness. When

Eddie died (S: stimulus), my C (consciousness) kicked in like crazy. One thing my C did was work on all that physiology stuff. But another bit of C had to figure out where or how all this fits into who I am, who we are and what we think matters. And do you know what I came up with? The absurd. Ultimately, it was absurd that Eddie died. There are physiological reasons for it. They're not absurd. Mentally, psychologically speaking, everything else about his death is absurd. As are everybody else's deaths, I think. That's why we must value life. And that's the paradox or, yes, my version of the 'meaning of life'!

This is where I've got to with my reflections. These reflections are now an S (stimulus) to you, which your C (consciousness) will act on before you come up with an R (response). At some point, if you talk to me, your R (response) will loop back and affect me via your C (consciousness). For example, you might alter my view that death (and Eddie's death) are absurd. Now there's a thought. I'm going to reflect on that.

SUGGESTION

Collect examples where you think there is stimulus response (as with someone hitting you just below your knee and your lower leg jumping into the air).

Now collect examples where you can see how the response comes from a base in reflection. Add to that examples where you can see that the person or thing delivering the stimulus is affected by your response. (Think of a game of tennis, for example.)

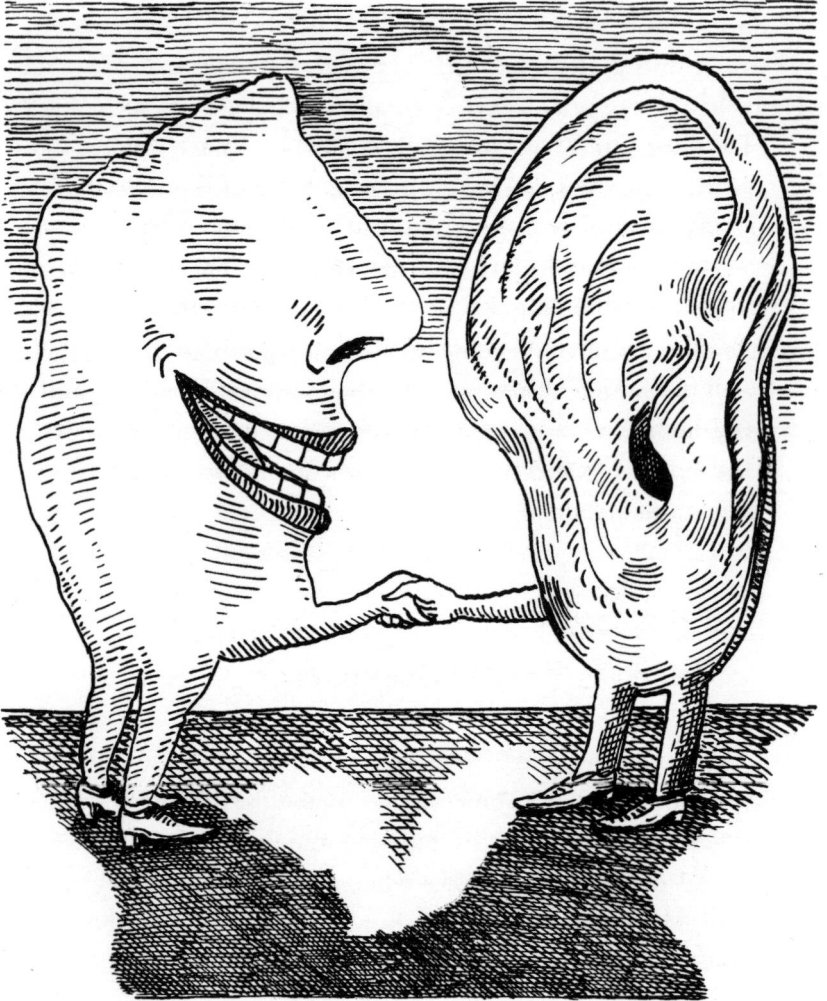

S

is for Speaking (and Listening)

The chair I'm sitting on to write this book is new. It has wheels, it can go up and down, it can swing round and round. I like it very much. I was sitting on it just a few hours before writing this page and there was a sudden cracking sound and it collapsed to the floor. Every bit of the mechanism holding the chair up, moved outwards and the seat part landed on the floor with me on top. It was pure slapstick. One moment, my head and body were above the table and a second later, my head and body were below the table. Buster Keaton would have been proud of me.

Emma came running in and said, 'What's happened?'

Still sitting on the seat on the floor, with my head at the level of the table, I said, 'The chair collapsed.'

Emma said, 'Why are you still sitting there?'

I said, 'Because I haven't got up.'

She pointed to the shelf above the table and said that the key to screw the screws in was there. I got up, reached for it, and we looked for the screws. We found three out of the four.

'We've got three,' Emma said.

'I'll look over here,' I said and I started feeling and looking over the floor.

I found it.

Emma tipped the chair upside down so that she could reattach the mechanism to the seat. Then she started screwing the screws into the plate that holds the chair and the mechanism together. She screwed two of them. We didn't say anything while she was doing this. She knew what to do. And I was propping up the seat.

Then she said, 'These two screws won't go in. It's like they're not lined up.'

I said, 'Maybe if you loosened the two you tightened up, we can swivel the plate round to line it up.'

She did that.

I waggled the chair.

'Careful!' she said.

Then the holes lined up and she tightened the screws. The chair was mended.

'You'll have to tighten the screws up every now and then to make sure it doesn't happen again,' she said.

'Mmm,' I said.

An everyday domestic scene. Two people, husband and wife, deal with a problem. We cooperate with the manhandling of the chair, we tell each other what needs to be done, we cooperate some more, the chair is mended. And there's some advice at the end.

I'm pretty sure that two animals, even chimpanzees, could not have done all of it, particularly the bit where between us we managed the problem of the holes not lining up and the advice that Emma gave me afterwards. One of these was about figuring out a way of solving the problem. (If that hadn't worked, we would have tried another way.) And the other is about projecting forwards into the future on the basis of what just happened, namely me dropping very suddenly to the floor. There's also just a hint of Emma's dry humour in the 'if you don't want it to happen again', as if there's the possibility that I might want it to happen again …? I acknowledge that with my 'Mmm'. (It's all in how we say it, I can assure you.)

Now I'm going to go all hyperbolic. This tiny scene is in microcosm how the human race has created civilisation and its enemy, total war. We've manhandled tools, made suggestions to each other, solved problems, and projected into the future. A key part of this has been speaking and listening.

Now, non-hyperbolically – that was great we did that. If that had happened when I was entirely on my own, I think that I might have tried to solve it, but in all likelihood I would have given up. Without the know-how, it needed four hands and some cooperative thought and action. It was the makings of a good day moment! If we are lucky, or have the knack or the sensitivity, this kind of speaking and listening is what makes for good times.

Of course, this is only one kind of speaking and listening. It's very operational and functional, though there are one or two personal bits going on too. We feel quite free to tell each what to do without either of us flying off the handle. As we all know, just one of those pieces of advice or instruction can be a cue for a row about tone of voice, an indication that this is part of a pattern of behaviour – so there might be an accusation about 'why do you always do that?', a defensive reply like 'no, I don't. It's you who can't bear me to do …', etc. We didn't go there. We didn't do that. Maybe it helped that it was a relatively simple job and that we both wanted the problem to be solved as simply and as quickly as possible.

Now, let me go to a very different situation. Paul, Head of English, has invited me to his school to talk to the whole of Year 7 (11- and 12-year-olds). That'll be about 200 school students. I prepare some poems to read and think for a while about what I'll say before I read them and how I'll link between them. I bear in mind something that I've learned from doing this – that there seems to be a magic barrier at precisely this age, where if I start by reading something that I think might be funny, the whole hour will go wrong. I can do that with 10- to 11-year-olds, but with 11-year-olds and older in secondary schools, it won't work. It's almost as if they're offended that I think I'm trying to be a comedian. So I've listened to reactions in similar situations and I've adapted what I say and what I read. I then plan the poems and chat for the hour.

I arrive at the school and it's strangely quiet. Paul is coming towards me across the playground. He says, 'Oh Mike, yeah, there's been a bit of a mix-up. Pretty well all the school is out on a trip. So we're going to be doing something a bit different. I've got the "remedial" class [as they used to be called! This was 40 years ago] in the library. They haven't gone on the trip.'

'OK,' I say, quickly thinking through my one-hour gig I had planned and wondering exactly what the word 'remedial' would entail. Should I take it all much more slowly? Are there things that I shouldn't say? I'm also assuming at this point that they will all be Year 7s. But I'm in for a surprise.

'Oh yeah, one other thing, Mike,' Paul says, 'it's cross-phase.'

'Cross-phase?'

'Sorry, yup, they're Year 7s to Year 11s. We're in the library. You'll be fine. It'll be great.' A picture comes up before me of a group of students, some of whom are tiny and worried, right up to some large, adult-sized 16-year-olds who know that they can and will leave school in a matter of weeks. I think to myself, *These are different kinds of human being. What the f— am I going to do?*

I'm fairly used to this kind of situation giving me 'shpilkes' – a Yiddish word literally meaning 'needles' – and the place these needles stick into you is your stomach. When you say, 'I've got shpilkes', you make a scooping shape with your hand and point it to your stomach. Along with shpilkes I was also getting 'dry tongue'. Dry tongue is what performers get and it's a trick invented by some kind of demon that hangs out with actors, which for some nasty reason makes your mouth and throat go dry so that you can't say the words. A nice demon would be helping you with this situation. This demon gives you dry tongue.

We carried on towards the library, Paul pushed open the door and, sure enough, exactly as I imagined it was a long table and all round it were about 20 school students ranging from the tiny to the huge. They looked at Paul and me. They seemed curious about me, with, I imagined, a slight touch of the usual leeriness from the oldest ones. They sensed, I thought, that this was a cock-up, and there's nothing better than seeing teachers sliding towards chaos.

Having been around schools a lot by this time, I knew that there can be tricky times to negotiate when younger and older students are put together. The younger ones can feel overawed, intimidated even, by the older ones. The older ones can feel demeaned by having to listen to stuff that is aimed at younger ones. It can all get quite abrasive. Experienced teachers know how to handle these things. I wasn't an experienced teacher. Far from it.

Paul introduced me. He said that I was a poet and we were going to have a great time. He was really sorry but he couldn't stay. Miss Rashid, the librarian, would be here though and off he went. I sat down. I picked up my most recent book, I thought of the poems in it about having a crash on my go-kart, getting up in the middle of the night and stealing the chocolate cake, me doing my toddler's nappy. They were all, every single one of them, completely wrong for this group. I was running through the playlist in my head. *There's the gag about … no, don't do any gags, Michael!*

I picked up the book, I put it down again and opened it at a random page. The page that fell open is a poem in which I talk about how my father, brother and I were going through the old photos, when I found a photo of my mother with a baby on her knee. I ask my father who it is, my brother or me?

My father says, it's neither of us, it's the baby who died. And this was the first time that either of us had ever heard about this baby. In the poem I wonder about the fact that my father mentioned this baby down through the years, but my mother never did. I then say, did that mean that she was more upset than my father or less? The poem doesn't answer the question. It hangs in the air.

So I read the poem to the group, thinking all the time of what would be the next poem that I could read, but before I did, one of the students had something to say. He was one of the older ones and he said that something like that had happened in his family. He told a story about a child who had died in his family. Then another student told a story about how his father had been in a very bad accident. Then another student told a story about how he had been in hospital.

And so it went on for the rest of the session. The students told stories. I think that after a while I suggested (or perhaps Paul came back and said it) that we write some of these stories down. As I said, this happened about 40 years ago and I've never forgotten it. I've never been in that situation before and I've always felt cautious about reading the poem or telling the story in front of the big audiences that I'm usually with these days. Perhaps I shouldn't be so cautious and just do it anyway!

But what was going on in this moment of speaking and listening? Why did the students feel so free to start telling me, a complete stranger, about these sad and awful things that had happened in their lives? And why were they so uninhibited about it?

Let's think of this geometrically. There was me, my story, the students and their stories. Lines pass between all four elements along which we share our experiences. One telling leads to another or 'triggers' another. In that space, we are finding aspects of our lives that we share. It may be that it's not the actual event of, say, being told about a baby who died, or a parent who had to go into hospital – it's the common feelings that we're sharing. We're selecting a feeling about an event and saying, 'I had that feeling too when the awful event in my family happened.' In this case, it might be feelings such as shock, sadness, loss. It might also be feelings about how we've coped since this sad event. We're comparing how we've each done that. After all, there's a sense that we're all looking at each other as the survivors.

Events themselves don't have feelings attached to them. What makes us human is that we have those feelings. When we come together and start talking, we are in a way researching whether my feelings are like your feelings are like his feelings are like her feelings … It's a very tentative, experimental time.

This means that talking is a way in which we acquire a bit of wisdom. It's wisdom about whether we are alone with these feelings or not, and it's wisdom about other people. How are they coping? How do they feel about such things?

As with my chair story, I'm going to be hyperbolic about this! I think this, in microcosm, is how we have created civilisation. We've talked and listened to each other – perhaps not enough – about pain and loss. This helps us cope with it. But it also sets up models for how we can or should treat each other. I have no idea whether those students had or had not previously been kind to each other in a 'cross-phase' situation but they certainly were that day. I think it was a good day for them. I hope but don't know that they carried away a memory of that day, into conversations and ways of treating people, in the future. And of course, it was a powerfully good day for me.

There's a picture by Quentin Blake in my *Sad Book* that always gives me a whooph in my stomach every time I look at it. It goes with my line, 'Sometimes I want to talk about all this with someone.' The picture shows a frantic-looking me, talking to someone who may be my mum or someone I'm hoping is my mum. The whooph comes from a cluster of feelings to do with remembering times when I wanted to talk about things with someone but couldn't, along with feelings to do with remembering times when I could and did, and how good that felt.

SUGGESTION

I probably don't need to suggest here that it's 'good to talk'. It's a cliché and anyway, sometimes it's not good to talk! What we have to find is times when it feels right to talk. Of course, some people are desperate to talk but they have no one to talk to. So another part of this suggestion is to try – sometimes, at the very least – to flip all this and make ourselves available to listen.

T

is for Tiggs

Tiggs was a cat. Except he wasn't called Tiggs.

I'll explain.

Once there was a cat called Mickie. My then six-year-old looked at Mickie and said, 'Does Mickie know she's a cat?' I didn't know the answer to that, but I can tell you that he went on to do Philosophy at university and got a distinction while doing an MA in it.

I put that down to Mickie.

Mickie died.

My stepdaughter took over. She noticed that a tabby cat was on the patio.

I said, 'Don't feed it; it'll want to come and stay.' So she fed it.

And the tabby came to stay. She called it Tiggs, because it looked like a tiger. I grew to be very fond of Tiggs. I like tabby cats. I agreed with my stepdaughter, it looked like a tiger. He also seemed to be very clever and very affectionate.

I remembered the cat that I had when I was growing up. My parents called it Simpkin. Simpkin is the cat in Beatrix Potter's book *The Tailor of Gloucester*. I loved Simpkin. He slept on my bed, though he did see ghosts. He would see them in the corner of the kitchen, arch his back, hiss at them and then run away. He was a cat who worried about things. One day Simpkin had babies but she had never objected to being Simpkin.

We gave all the kittens away but one. My parents called this one Archy after the cat in the story *Archy and Mehitabel*. I read the story, and Archy wasn't a cat. Archy was a cockroach. The cat is called Mehitabel. I wondered if Archy minded being named after a cockroach. No, he never objected to being Archy the cockroach. All that was long before Tiggs.

Back with my stepdaughter: one day, she made friends with the girl down the road. The friend came over for tea. She saw Tiggs and said, 'That's Billy.' My stepdaughter said it was Tiggs.

'No,' said the friend. 'Billy was my cat but one day he disappeared.'

I was ashamed and said nothing, but my stepdaughter was quite proud. 'Yes,' she said, 'I fed him.'

My stepdaughter grew up and now has two cats. She said to me that she was going to call one of them Misty. I said, 'That reminds me of the Clint Eastwood film, *Play Misty for Me*. It doesn't end well,' I said.

My stepdaughter called the cat Misty.

Cats taught my son philosophy and my stepdaughter self-will.

Back to the time of Tiggs. One day, in the time of Tiggs (Billy), another cat turned up on the patio.

I said to my stepdaughter, 'Don't feed it, or it'll stay', so she fed it.

The children discussed what to call it. They decided that it should be called Smudge, named after the Arsenal striker Alan 'Smudger' Smith. It didn't look like Smudger. For a start, it was a 'she' and it was blue and had a little moustache. One of the children called it Hitler but I said that wasn't nice, so he went on calling it Hitler.

One day, I was invited to a wedding. The groom asked all the guests to line up for a photo. I found myself standing next to the great Arsenal striker, several times winner of the Golden Boot for the most goals scored in one season, Alan 'Smudger' Smith. As we stood side by side, I said, without turning my head towards him (not wanting to spoil the photo), 'We named our cat after you.'

Alan Smith has a very deadpan, Midlands accent.

He said, without looking at me, 'Is he nippy?'

I said, 'No, she isn't.'

We went on posing for the photo.

He then said, still without looking at me, eyes fixed on the camera, 'I once heard of someone naming their goldfish after me, but never a cat.'

I went home and told the family and they were very proud of both Smudges.

One day some other neighbours came over. They looked at Smudge and said, 'That's Molly.'

My stepdaughter said, 'No, that's Smudge.'

My son said, 'That's Hitler.'

The neighbour said that Smudge was their cat and it was Tiggs's aunt. I didn't tell Alan Smith about that. My step-daughter went on feeding Smudge (Molly).

For reasons that are wound up with how humans behave – rather than cats – two more cats arrived. Emma explained that these cats were her cats and they were named after two gangsters: Tony Soprano and Benny Blanco.

They were two ginger toms – brothers – and very much in love with each other. They followed each other round the house, licked each other and slept together. I asked Emma why they licked each other.

She said, 'Because they're brothers.'

I said, 'I don't lick my brother.' I never got to the bottom of that.

As it were.

Then Tiggs died. He chose to die under a stationary car. I was very sad. Smudge died soon after. We figured she was sad that Tiggs had died. It was the most sympathetic thing she had ever done, as she hadn't been very friendly to Tiggs even though she was his aunt, or Hitler.

We moved house with the loving gangsters. When Tony died, Benny went looking for him. Up till then, he had had only one kind of miaow. Whenever one cat was outside and the other cat was in, the one inside called to the one outside to come in.

'Come in,' he'd say, 'don't hang about out there.'

After Tony died, he carried on with that miaow but every now and then he went to the door and did a completely different miaow. It was a long, low grumble. It was heartbreaking.

Then Benny died.

I thought that it was time for a break from cats. Everyone disagreed. I said that we could have a cat, but only if we got a cat flap. That was my bottom line. No cat flap, no cat. Everyone agreed.

One day Emma went off to Brighton with our daughter. She said that they might bring back a cat.

I said, 'No cat flap, no cat.'

They said, 'Not even one little tiny kitten?'

I said, 'OK, then, one little tiny kitten.' They came back with a box.

They opened it up.

Inside were two kittens.

I said, 'That's not one cat. That's two cats.'

They said, 'One kitten would have been lonely.'

'And we haven't got a cat flap,' I said.

'No,' they said.

They're black and white.

I said, 'One of them is dozy, and the other one is nervous. Let's call the dozy one Shlump [pronounced 'shloomp' – Yiddish for an untidy, slack sort of a person], and the nervy one Shpilkes [as we saw in S is for Speaking, this is Yiddish for needles, meaning nerves]'.

They said that they look as if they've got white stripes, so they didn't name them Shlump and Shpilkes, they named them after the people in the band The White Stripes – Meg and Jack.

I said, 'You'll need to bond with Meg and Jack. It's called "imprinting".'

They said, 'Yes, you should.'

So I picked them up and stroked them.

They now think I'm mummy. Meg does it in a shlumpy way and sits on me whenever she can, and Jack does it nervily as if he's got shpilkes.

They talk to me. I talk to them. I write the conversations down. They talk at the same time as each other, in unison.

Cats: You're at home today.

Me: Yep.

Cats: What? All day?

Me: Yep.

Cats: Not going out at all?

Me: Nope.

Cats: Can't you think of something to do out there where you usually go?

Me: Nope.

Cats: Fine. Ruin our day, then.

Me: Just by my being here?

Cats: Yep. You've said it.

Later:

Cats: Look at us!

Me: Could you mind out the way? I'm on a Zoom call.

Cats: We know! Cooee! It's us! Hello, people!

Me: I'm on a serious work call here. Please move!

Cats: Hey you on the screen, what do you think of our bums?

Me: Oh please!

Cats: We're so lovely, aren't we?

Me: No.

Even later:

Cats: We're going to destroy the rug.

Me: Please don't.

Cats: Too late. We're doing it.

Me: But why?

Cats: We don't like the pattern.

Me: Mm?

Cats: To create great art, first we must destroy the art of what has come before.

Me: All you're doing is scratching a rug.

Cats: Fool.

Yet later:

Cats: We're not going out there.

Me: I'm not sending you out there.

Cats: You looked at us as if you thought we should be out there.

Me: I was just looking out there.

Cats: First you looked at us, then you looked out there.

Me: So?

Cats: You're obsessed with out there.

Bedtime:

Cats: We didn't vote for Trump.

Me: But you don't vote for anyone.

Cats: Trust you to turn this into a political attack on us.

Me: I was just pointing out that you don't have a vote.

Cats: Exactly. And that's why we're in the mess we're in.

Me: Can I think about that for a moment?

Cats: What's that you're eating?

Me: Lettuce.

Cats: Why do you eat it? Lettuce is pointless. It's green.

Me: I've seen you eat green stuff. You eat grass.

Cats: That's so we can sick up stuff when you give us
      rubbish cat food. Does lettuce make you sick?

Me: No.

Cats: So it's pointless.

Me: England won.

Cats: Won what?

Me: The game. England v Netherlands.

Cats: Does that matter?

Me: In terms of the history of the world, no.

Cats: In terms of the history of cats?

Me: Er ...

Cats: We'll take that as a no.

Me: Can you just run with my enthusiasm on this?

Cats: No.

Me: Have you seen my phone?

Cats: No.

Me: I'm sure I left it on the desk here.

Cats: Really?

Me: Oh look, it's on the floor under the desk.

Cats: It must have jumped off the desk onto the floor.

Me: I wonder if an animal pushed it off the desk.

Cats: Highly unlikely.

Me: Really?

Me: Why don't you get a job?

Cats: Why don't *you* get a job?

Me: I work.

Cats: But it's not a job, is it? You just shuffle bits of
    paper and push us off your computer.

Me: That shuffling is creative.

Cats: Not as creative as us sitting around.

Me: What do you create?

Cats: Vibes.

Cats: You haven't been here.

Me: True.

Cats: Explain yourself.

Me: We were in France.

Cats: Were you with cats?

Mc: No.

Cats: Did you see cats?

Me: Yes, I saw one in a window.

Cats: Did you stroke it?

Me: I was outside, the cat was inside.

Cats: Good. Don't go away again.

Me: What are you staring at?

Cats: Our sick.

Me: You should be clearing it up.

Cats: That's your job.

Me: You could eat it.

Cats: Do you eat your sick?

Me: No.

Cats: Well, don't expect us to do what you wouldn't do yourself.

Me: Is that your philosophy?

Cats: The only way is ethics.

Cats: There you go.

Me: It's four in the morning.

Cats: Yep.

Me: What's that?

Cats: Your 'To Do' list.

Me: You've brought it up from downstairs and put it by the bed?

Cats: Yep.

Me: It's four in the morning.

Cats: Yep.

Me: I don't need reminding of what to do at four in the morning.

Cats: You do.

Cats.

Happy days.

So why do we have cats? Why do we have pets?

What would I say to a Martian who knocked on my door, came in and said, 'What are they?'

'Cats,' I say.

'What are they doing here?' the Martian says.

And I say, 'Er ...'

What do I say?

Because they're interesting? Comforting? Strange? Because I can express feelings with them that I can't express with human beings?

'Like what?' says the Martian.

'Now that's a very personal question,' I say.

'Yes,' says the Martian. 'Back on Mars I'm a psychotherapist.'

'Well,' I say, 'perhaps I'm not brilliant at saying, "I love you." Perhaps I'm not brilliant at always making sure that the "other person" is OK. Look, I don't want to go on with you probing me about this.'

'Yes,' says the Martian, in a loaded sort of way.

'OK,' I say, 'I like the way they show their devotion.'

'I see,' says the Martian, 'so it's all about you.'

'No,' I say, 'it's all about the pet.'

'I think you need to think about that,' says the Martian.

Indeed I do. And am.

SUGGESTION

If you haven't got a pet (or pets) you can ignore all this.

If you have, it's fun to muse about these things, isn't it?

And why not have a go at writing conversations with them? Or even acting them out with children, friends, relatives!

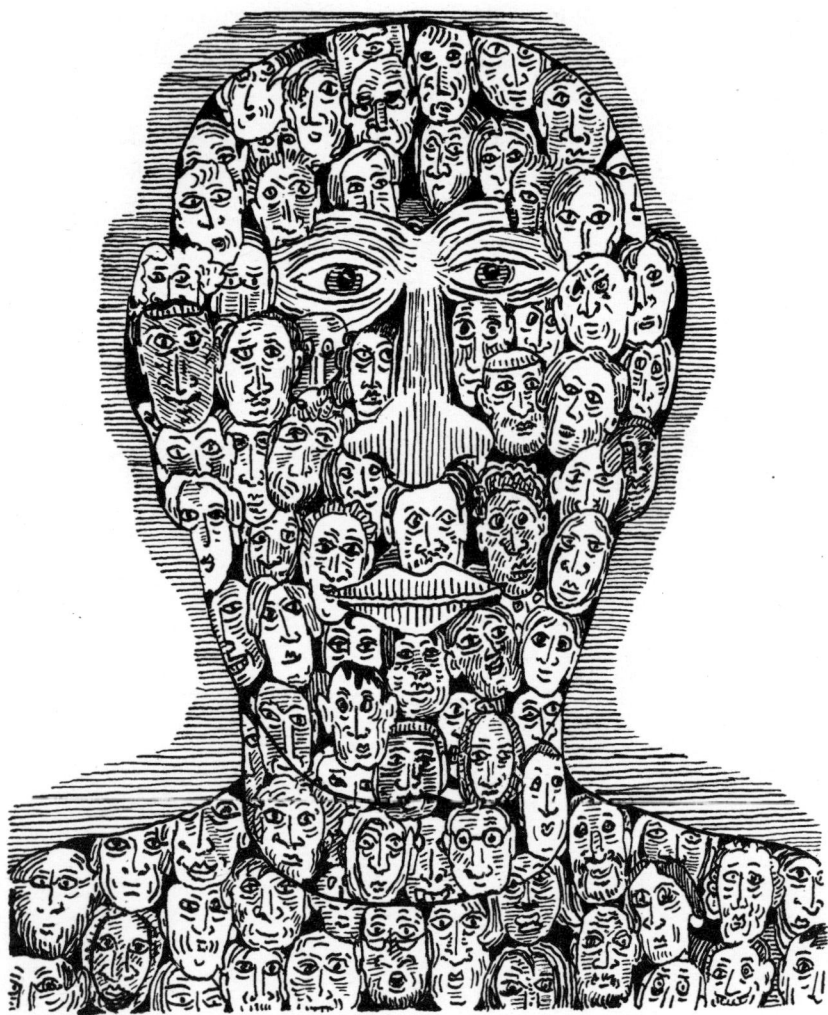

U

is for Union

My mother is opening an envelope at the breakfast table. She pulls out a piece of paper and, with an ironic look on her face, turns to me and my brother and says, with a triumphant edge to her voice, 'I'm four-sevenths of your father!'

At the time, I don't think I fully understood what she was talking about and it took some explaining. The National Union of Teachers (the NUT) campaigned for many years for equal pay for women teachers. The National Association of School Masters (the NAS, as I think it was called then) opposed it. It was a bitter fight and it divided staffrooms and families, but in the end the NUT and other trade unions won the argument and convinced the government to put it in place but … with one proviso: equal pay couldn't be implemented in one go. It had to be implemented in 'seven increments', each one added on annually. So it was that I remember my mother's exultant cry on this particular morning, indicating that she had reached a point where her pay was calculated on the basis of being four-sevenths of what a man would have received.

In fact, I suspect it wouldn't have been exactly four-sevenths of our father's salary on account of him having taught for more years than our mother, but let's leave that technicality to one side. I should add here that my father was also an active member of the NUT and had supported the campaign for equal pay. I dread to think what our household would have been like if he had been in the NAS. A moment like this one, with the 'sevenths' rising, would have ended up being an almighty domestic clash over the corn flakes.

Someone with more knowledge of trade union history would be able to tell me exactly what year this was, and – to be absolutely honest with you – it might have been an earlier seventh than the four-sevenths! The point here, though, is two things: my mother's triumph about a future in which her salary would be calculated on an equal basis but also the fact that she was part of a movement that had won it. I should dive in here and say that a bitter moment came for her when she applied for a primary school headship and was told that in the locality where she had always taught, they didn't appoint women as headteachers. Even worse, the headteacher who they did appoint became a frequent visitor to our house to get into deep discussion with my mother to ask her for advice as to how best to proceed with this or that bit of school policy. I can hear her saying goodbye to him at the door and coming back into the room, gnashing her teeth!

It was a lesson in how a victory on one front can turn into a knockback on another.

It wasn't the first time our parents had talked of collective action and victories. The big one for them had been what has come to be known as the 'Battle of Cable Street' of 1936. They were 17 years old and had not long been a 'courting couple'. The 'battle' was about the fact that Oswald Mosley and the British Union of Fascists announced that they were going to march down Cable Street, in the heart of what was then a largely Jewish area in the East End of London. My parents (Harold Rosen and Connie Isakofsky, as they were then) were both Jewish East Enders and on the day were part of a huge street demonstration that gathered to stop the march going ahead.

As with the 'four-sevenths' announcement, the way that I heard about this day was at the kitchen table, with my mother moving cups and jugs round to show my brother and me who was where and when – a domestic version of Churchill's War Cabinet table, I guess.

What happened on this day was that so many people came out onto the street, that the police tried to force a path through the crowd, so that the BUF could march through. For several hours there were pitched battles between the police and local people, while the BUF waited a few streets away. (Mind you, I've seen a lot of footage of this day and there are moments when several BUF men join the police in attacking the demonstrators.) In the end, the police told Oswald Mosley and the others that they couldn't clear the way for them to march, and the BUF 'went home'.

When my mother told the story it was full of much more colour than this, with stories of barricades made of beds, tables and chairs, a tram or a bus getting 'stuck' in the street on account of a sympathetic driver who got out of his cab and 'disappeared', a 'spy who stood with the BUF and reported back on what they were doing' … and so on. Without wanting to trivialise it, I think I got it that in a way, this was Harold and Connie's first date!

When Mum told the story, there was also a non-heroic aspect to it. Cable Street is a long, narrow street with a set of small side streets off it. The 'defence' of Cable Street was to block off the street with barricades and also to block off the side streets too, so the BUF couldn't wangle their way into Cable Street down one of these side entries. H and C (as they sometimes called themselves) found themselves in one of these side streets, but, somehow or another, on the wrong side of the barricades. Instead of standing behind the barricade, they were in front of it. Mum described the scene of the narrow street, groups of people behind the barricade, people leaning out of windows, everyone talking, shouting and singing – but there stood my parents on the empty patch of road in front of the barricade.

At that moment, some mounted police appear at the end of the street, coming towards H and C. There is nowhere for them to go. They are trapped in the narrow street with the barricade behind them. They are almost certainly going to be coshed or worse – which they had seen happening to people for several hours before then. A lot of people got badly injured that day. What are they going to do? They turned towards the barricade and backed against the wall of the street, hoping to avoid being run over by the 'mounties'' horses.

When you're eight years old, this was exciting stuff for a teatime kitchen table talk. Your mother, a respectable suburban primary school teacher, who goes off to work every day in her smartest clothes, is telling you a story about a day on the streets, taking place in what always seemed like a strange, mythic place and time, 'the East End in the 1930s'.

So what happened to them? A door in one of the houses opened, and they were pulled in and out of the way of the mounted police. Whenever my parents told the story, they turned it into an ironic tale of how they had ended up 'on the wrong side of the barricades'. Bit by bit, over the years, I got it that they were playing with the metaphorical meaning of that phrase, what with it usually being a jibe about traitors and enemies not supporting the revolution! The joke only worked because anyone listening to them tell the story knew that their support for the defence of the East End was of course total.

What wasn't total was a defeat for the BUF or indeed for fascism. As with my mother and the equal pay win, I got it from my parents that you might win something but it won't be all. Fascism didn't win in Britain, but it won in Italy, Spain and Germany and by 1942, it looked very much as if it was going to engulf the whole of Europe. As my mother said, if Hitler had won, we (my brother and me) 'wouldn't be here'. She was saying that with the knowledge of those days in 1945 and 1946 when the first news reports came through about the concentration and extermination camps and my father talked of relatives in France and Poland who were 'there before the war, but who weren't there at the end of the war'.

The kitchen table, then, was a place where I learned a lot about these wins and losses. It explains why my mother behaved the way she did during the 'bus strike' of May and June 1958. By then I was at grammar school, aged 12, and for many of us, a bus journey was essential. We lived three miles or so from school. Teachers and parents ferried the school students to school. I got a lift in the maths teacher's Morris Minor, and given that I was hopeless at maths, the journeys were a bit tense. Pretty soon, the conversation in the playground and at 'register time' was around allegedly over-paid bus drivers holding Londoners to ransom. I came home repeating some of this. My mother said, 'You'll have to put some money in the bucket.'

'What bucket?'

'There'll be a bucket outside Harrow Weald Bus Garage, so that you can show support for them.'

'How do you know there'll be a bucket?'

'There's always a bucket. It's for the strike fund. To support the people out on strike. They're not getting paid.'

So, that day, after school, I missed my ride home with Mr Ponsford and went down to the bus garage. I walked over to the entrance and there was a man sitting there (the 'picket') and next to him was a bucket. Mum was right. He looked at me (12 years old in my grammar-school uniform, cap on my head). I bent down and put a 'ten bob' note in the bucket. (Ten shillings – in other words, half a pound.)

I'm not sure how I got home that night (or on the other nights that I put some money in the bucket) but my mother wanted me to know that this is 'what we do'.

Sitting here in my seventies, I could go on and on telling stories like this, and fill it in with anything and everything I've read about trade unions, communal self-defence or demonstrations in support of a campaign – wins and losses. It's OK, I won't. But once when I was quite young, a teenager I think, I asked my father: what is a trade union? He said that he had once asked his 'zeyde' (Yiddish for grandfather) that same question and his zeyde talked to him about a box of matches. English was Zeyde's second or even third language, with Yiddish and Polish being his first two. My father imitated him affectionately. He adored his zeyde, partly on account of my father growing up not having a father at home with him. Zeyde took on a fatherly role but, sadly, my father lost him when he was only 13.

So my father would say, 'Zeyde told me, "Voss is a union? A union is a box o' matches. One match – you can break. Two matches – you can break. Three matches – you can break. But take a whole box o' matches – you can't break. That is voss is a union."'

When my father's zeyde was talking about this, he was pulling it out of his past in the struggles for wages and equality for Polish Jewish workers in the 1880s and '90s. In case I should ever think of these things as trapped in black-and-white films of people moving about jerkily a hundred years ago, the present day is in many ways no different. I teach at a university that seems to be constantly considering or actually firing people. At times like this, I see colleagues who have spent years building up qualifications and experience, working in teams to create departments committed to a subject and a way of working, sweating away out of hours, writing articles and books to achieve the right 'publish or perish' levels, only to hear that they are going to be fired in a few months' time. Rents, mortgages and the welfare of their families are on the line. People walk about with a sense of their life ambitions and self-worth going down the pan. They ask themselves, didn't I do what education told me to do? Work hard, pass every exam with flying colours, do research, get 'approved', get a job ... only to find that it's worth nothing? You can see that it's both a financial and a personal blow. It feels as if a chunk of the education system is breaking and you are right at the point of the break. It's you that's being broken.

I haven't had that experience directly because I'm a part-timer and I have other ways of earning money. Even so, I received notice that my job was 'possibly' in the frame for being removed. I did think to myself, *Why have I spent ten years co-devising and co-teaching a course (an MA in Children's Literature) that has developed some unique ideas and practices?* (We are one of the only courses that I have heard of that enables MA students to devise research projects in which they investigate how children respond to books. So instead of it being adults explaining why this or that children's book is good or bad, children say or write about what they think. Seems like a valuable thing to do to me!)

Anyway, in order to fight for my job, I was told that I would have to fill in a long form explaining why I thought that what I do was good ... or some such. I couldn't resist going public with this, and conjured up a picture of me telling management how I rated *We're Going on a Bear Hunt*. I then heard that management quietly dropped me having to evaluate myself, only to hear soon after that our key member of staff (let's call her Mary) was in the frame to be fired. When I say 'key', I really do mean that if Mary went, our whole MA course would fold. It really wouldn't be possible to carry on without her.

Again came that sense of futility and loss.

But, as you might guess, we have a union, the UCU, and at every stage in the process of losing hundreds of jobs, we have tried to draw a line in the sand and say, enough is enough. It's been five years or so of rearguard, defensive action, trying to secure people's jobs, winning the best 'severance' deals possible and so on. There have been long, bitter strikes, which we hate doing because it undermines the whole basis on which we work in university, which is to give people a great education and improved life chances – particularly so in the university where I teach, which has had a high proportion of students who are the first in their family to go to university, or are from diverse backgrounds, many of them from families who came to this country from abroad.

In one of the ultimatums we gave management, after losing scores of staff, we said that we would go on strike again and withhold all marking of finals exams if they sacked the group of teachers that Mary was part of. There was a stand-off. We waited. Then we heard that we won that one. Mary stays. Our course is safe. For the time being.

Every time I work alongside Mary (we team teach), I think how this is only possible because we did manage to draw that line in the sand over the group of staff that Mary was in whom we fought for. It's not just about hanging on to jobs (why not?! That's worthy in itself) but about what we believe is something of quality that we offer to people wanting to develop their teaching, in order then to benefit the children they teach.

There are several philosophies behind all this. There's the principle expressed by my great-grandfather and the box of matches: if we stick together, you can't break us down. But behind that there's a view of the self and the other. That sounds pompous but just take this last example of Mary. If we are just individuals, bobbing about like little coloured balls in a jar, then it really doesn't matter about Mary. 'Sorry you gotta go, an' all that, but you're clever, you'll find something else to do and if push comes to shove, you can go and work in a shop, or something … In the meantime, I'm over here, I've gotta look after my life.'

This is a view that sees 'me' as being a self-created, self-driven, self-reliant, totally 'individuated' being. To be fair, much of this book speaks to this side of ourselves. That's because I believe that we can hold two ideas in our heads about this: we can do what we can (up to a point) to take care of ourselves, but we are always created by – and we are part of creating – the social groups we live and work with and beyond into society as a whole. Here's an example: I am alive because in 2020 teams of people cooperated and struggled to keep me alive, in an institution, the NHS, which millions of people like my parents and grandparents fought for, so that we could all look after each other. I can look at myself, as a 'me', doing my exercises to learn how to walk again, and yet there were physiotherapists and occupational therapists helping me to help myself. It was an 'us'. Even my body – and we often think of our bodies as being highly personal, individual things – was in effect owned by teams of doctors, nurses and therapists, pumping air and drugs into me in the hope that my own antibodies might neutralise the Covid virus.

Even the way we talk is formed through our social inter-actions, using words and phrases developed over hundreds of years of millions more social interactions.

This may seem far away from U is for Union but I'll claim it isn't! When we see ourselves as part of others, and others as part of us, then the idea of a union (or the NHS) is a logi-cal necessity.

SUGGESTION

Join a union.

(I didn't need to say that, did I?!)

When (!) you join a union, don't be put off by the regulations, rules and procedures. Though they seem incomprehensible and annoying at first, they are there for very good reasons. They safeguard people's rights. Never be afraid to ask what the abbreviations and terms mean. What are 'standing orders'? What does it mean to 'take that amendment'? Ask, ask, ask. If you don't believe me about procedures, then try being in a meeting that has no procedures. They're fun and great to start off with and then quickly turn into ego-trips for very few people, people talking too long, people being excluded and so on.

That said, unions are not perfect. There are all sorts of things going on in them that you might find are not satisfactory. If so, find out how these matters can be raised.

Within unions there are 'factions' and 'fractions'. You might find that you want to be part of one of them. Or very much not!

In and around unions, we discover people of similar views, similar outlooks. This is all part of what we hope will be progress, whether on pay, conditions, support or solidarity. Good days stuff, in fact.

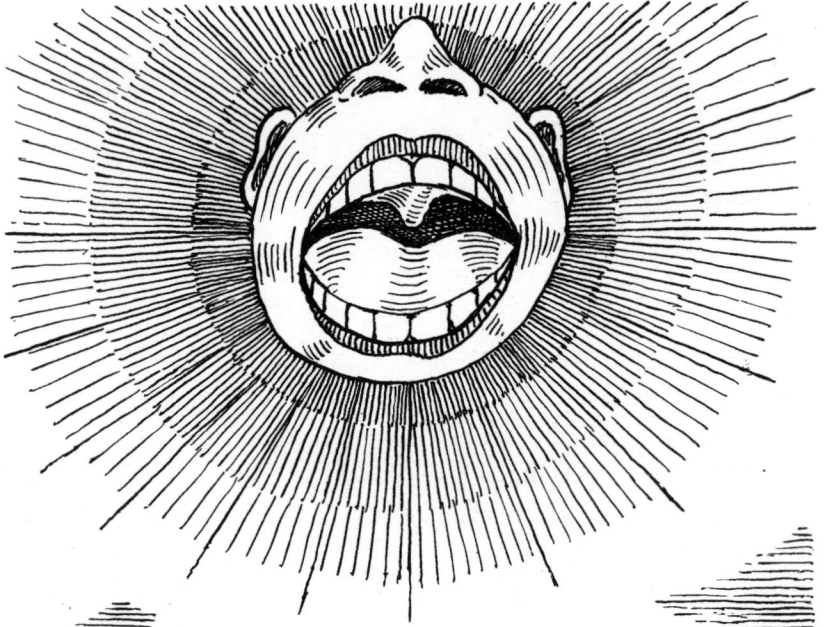

V

is for Van Morrison

This is not going to be a plea for you all to love Van Morrison. I am not even going to claim that loving Van Morrison is your key to having a good day.

Just in case you don't know, Van Morrison is an Irish singer from Northern Ireland who has been playing and singing in bands since 1957 when he was 12. If you don't know of him or have never heard him, that's fine. If you have heard him and don't like his stuff, that's fine too.

What I'm talking about here is a way of listening. Nearly all of us like listening to some kind of music. Trying to explain why we do this is quite hard, though. I guess there's a good reason for why it's hard. You could almost say that the point of a good deal of music is that it expresses things that we can't say in words. If we could express in words all that music does for us, there wouldn't be much point in having music! It's as if there's a place in our brains allocated to the feeling of music, and it's a place that the wordy part of our brain can't get to. Another way of looking at it is to say that I've found that though there are some kinds of music that I can say a few things about, there are others that – even if I can say a few things about them – there really isn't much point: just let the music do the talking.

And this takes me to Van Morrison. For you, it might be someone else – another composer, singer, orchestra, band, etc. So I can say something about the style of Van Morrison. I can say something about what kind of tradition of music he seems to be part of. But saying such things doesn't say anything at all about why I like hearing him and the bands and singers he plays with. What I really like doing is getting to a place which, when listening to him, I can't say why I'm enjoying it. Philosophers have words for this feeling – words like 'inexpressible', 'ineffable' and 'sublime'.

At the risk of harming this feeling, we can ask ourselves, what is our own personal and cultural route to these sublime moments? That's because patterns and styles of music come to us bearing traditions. We only have to try to hear a music from a tradition that we've never or hardly ever heard before, and we might well find that it can't give us those ineffable and sublime moments. Right now, I could make two lists: on one side I could put the musical traditions where I find those sublime moments and on the other side I could list some musical traditions that don't do it for me. I'm not going to do it, because I know that such lists make people annoyed. And it is annoying to be told by someone that the music you adore just doesn't cut the mustard for them! And again, that's not the point of this chapter. The point is to celebrate the joy in seeking out the sublime.

What I'm saying then is that the sublime is mysterious and inexpressible in itself, but the roots of the particular music we love are not necessarily so mysterious. In the case of Van Morrison (who we fans call 'Van the Man' (!)), he has himself been very keen to tell us about the music he heard at home, and the people who influenced his voice, the tunes he composes and how he performs. For me, that's part of the pleasure, feeling the roots coming through as he performs – in his case, traditions like gospel, blues, soul and the like. But saying this is the wordy stuff, not the sublime. For the sublime to happen, I find it's a good idea for me to switch off the wordy stuff. And this is it: there's a particular kind of wordless immersion that does the trick. It's as if you have to give yourself over to the music, submitting to it, or even surrendering to it. Very good day sort of stuff.

I find that this takes time. I'm only a bit musical. It takes me a long time to learn a tune. When I sing, I frequently sing flat. When I try to keep a beat, my musician friends tell me that I 'drift to the offbeat'. I could once read music but it was only just about well enough to play a recorder at school, and I can't do that any more. I did teach myself how to play the harmonica in a blues style but I didn't ever get myself into a band or with a singer/guitar-player. Perhaps this all explains the reason why I find certain kinds of music – like Van Morrison – out of reach, mysterious even. Another example: the first time I heard Bob Marley, I couldn't figure out how this wonderful sound was made. I couldn't figure out how the sound of the band (The Wailers) was put together. What combination of instruments produced those sounds? In that sense, it was a music I couldn't 'read', but instead of this resulting in me blocking it out (or not being able to find a way in), it just 'happened' for me. I could say the same for some American 'bluegrass' music, Irish fiddle and uilleann pipe music, Miles Davis … I won't go on!

What I've taught myself to do is what I call 'sitting in'. If I hear a tune, a voice, a band, a sound that catches my ear, I give myself the space to 'sit in' with it. This means playing it over and over again. Quite often, for this to be that sublime moment, I will find that I can't imitate it. I can't sing it or whistle it, or play it on the harmonica. All I can do with it is to let it go into my mind and for my mind to feel around it as if I'm stroking a cat with my eyes shut.

There are also ideal times and conditions for it, and these have changed across my life. Right now, it's on my own, later at night, finding live performances online. In the past, it might have been in small clubs hearing an instrumentalist, a group or a singer who I could see and hear just a few feet away.

Van Morrison has produced many records, played with many different musicians, appeared on TV and there's plenty of him on YouTube. He also does many live shows all over the world. The live shows are a real curiosity. He often gives off a vibe of being irritated with the audience, the band or the backing singers. He may even interrupt the show in the middle of a song and shout to the audience words to the effect of, 'This is live music! Don't expect it to sound like it does on the record,' and you can see him 'arranging' the music right there on stage in front of you. When he gives this little speech, he does it as if he's pretty annoyed with the audience, as if we had just shouted, 'Play it like it is on the record, Van!' The other great thing about the speech is when he delivers it, we regular Van the Man aficionados cheer.

This all adds to the mystique, as if we have some personal relationship or attachment to Van the Man, and because some of the songs are themselves mysterious, elliptical and suggestive rather than literal and obvious, this mystique feeds into something about Van the Man and his music that I find I can't grasp. Interestingly, he has his own words for this: 'the inarticulate speech of the heart' – which is both the title and one of the repeated choruses of one of his songs.

One of Van's frustrations, though, is trying to get the bands who he plays with to play the music in the way that he wants them to. As far as I can make out, when he's on tour, he frequently works with local bands. He clearly wants there to be an improvisational, spontaneous quality about this – and I've seen recordings of concerts in the States or in Germany, say, where he's happy. On the other hand, there's one song that seems to bother him. It's called 'Into the Mystic', and it's a mix of a love song and a homecoming (I think!) – and as you can hear with that title, it has him trying to express the inexpressible. However, there's one key literal bit of the song where he sings about the foghorn blowing as he's coming home. On the record, there's a wonderful deep bass note that both imitates a foghorn and fits in the 'hole' in the song between the lines. Here's the funny bit: when he plays live with bands, you can see him on the videos cueing up the foghorn sound but, time after time, you can see bands hitting a duff sound or wrong note, so that mournful, nostalgic, loving feeling is missed. In turn, this brings out the irritation in Van, and you can see him venting his frustration or trying to find an instrument for himself to play the note, the next time it comes round in the song.

Again, this all adds to the mystique (not the 'mystic'!) of what it is he's trying to do with his music. I imagine that he's spent a good deal of his musical life looking for ways to create the 'mystic' or the 'inarticulate speech of the heart' and for me, there are definitely times he finds it, makes it and shares it.

I've talked about how we can 'sit in' these times, but at other times, isn't there something consoling about them? This is hard to describe and express too. We might feel down, sad, depressed even. We might feel (as I have) that I had emotions in me that I couldn't describe, but these ineffable, sublime moments in music seem to be able to 'chime' with them. The word 'consoling' feels like the right way to describe this. Something of the rawness or the hurt can be lessened or 'melted' by certain tunes, musicians or performances. And we deserve to be consoled! We humans have lumbered ourselves with feelings of loss, unrequited or impossible affections, regrets, hurtful memories, unfulfilled hopes, anxieties and much more, and certain kinds of music can 'house' or 'contain' these feelings for us. It's as if they beckon us and say, 'Sit with this for a while. It may feel as if the music is giving your feelings a voice.' The sadness, hurt or regret may feel as if the music is expressing it. And yet, I wonder, how can it do that? I might be able to name what notes, what instruments or what rhythms can do that for me, but that doesn't say exactly how those sounds connect with our minds and console me.

You can hear Van Morrison's lyrics (or read them online) and even when he's trying to find the inexpressible, his words usually make sense. Some singers and traditions are deliberate ways of not making sense. Such music seems to sit between the non-sense of instrumental music and the sense of song lyrics. In the folk tradition, one example of this from Scotland is an a cappella singing of what is known as 'mouth music'. A modern band that aimed to do this was the Cocteau Twins, in particular on the album *Heaven or Las Vegas*. You can hear words and phrases but there is no coherent sense to the lyrics. It's another kind of mouth music but instead of it being a cappella there is a rich and mysterious instrumental accompaniment. If I try to find words for it, I come up with things like 'uncanny', 'bizarre', 'stirring' and the like, but these really are inadequate terms. They don't get anywhere near to how I've felt listening over and over (as I have) to the songs.

Again, this is not about me telling you to listen to the album! It's more of a praise-song for the process: that one way to make for a good time or a good day is to seek out these sublime moments in music. In case this seems obvious, I'm reminded of the moment in John Mortimer's play *A Voyage Round my Father* when the father character says in an angry, spitting sort of a way, 'I … hate … music!' I often hear that line in my mind, because when Eddie died, I couldn't bear to listen to music. I couldn't stand the way that music seemed at that time to be attacking me, invading, inveigling its way into my mind, in order to bother me and upset me. Then, at some point, I could listen to Van the Man, Bob Marley and my other sublime musics again.

Why was that? How was it impossible at one point and then possible later? I don't know. Asking those questions is part of the ineffable quality that I've been trying to grasp in this chapter. As you might suspect, part of me doesn't want to examine it and explain it, in case I lose the ability to have it. As with the music itself, I can 'sit in' a space in which it's OK for it to be mysterious.

SUGGESTION

There's a piece of music out there waiting for you to love it.

Though I want you to keep reading this book, I'm tempted to ask you to put it down and go and listen to that music NOW.

Yes, I am going to ask you to do it, in spite of losing you.

Do it.

Now.

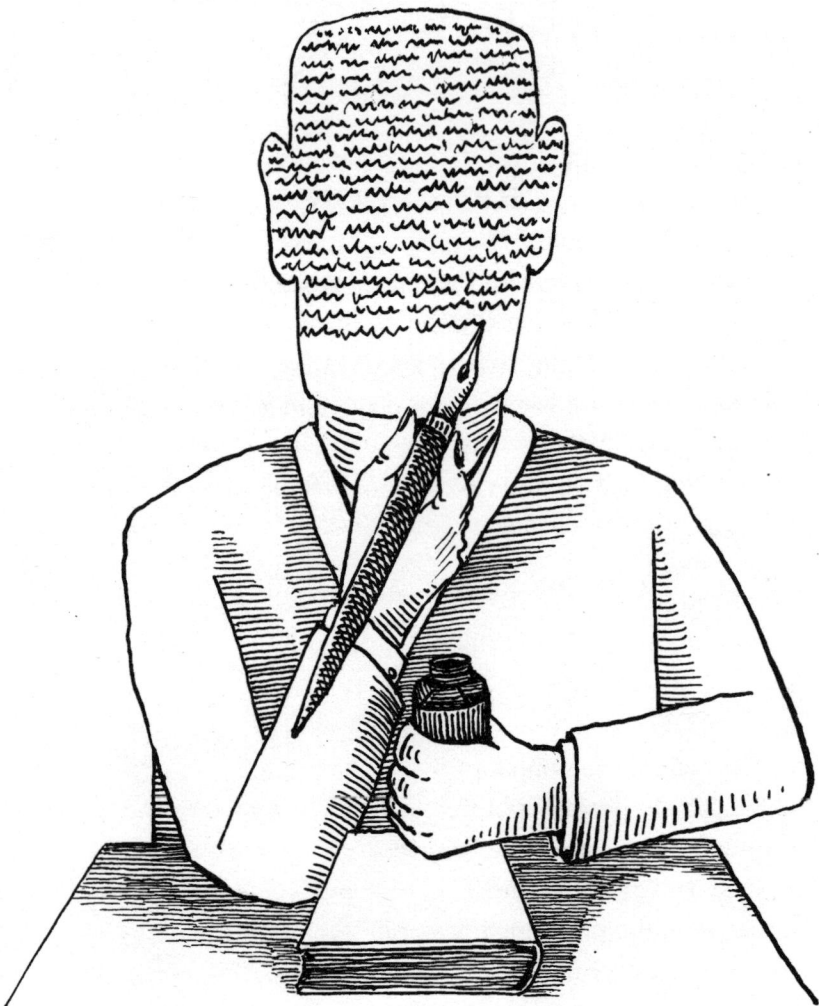

W

is for Writing

Someone is stuck up a tree. How do they get out of it?

This is a jokey way in which somebody (I'm not sure who) described the essence of the beginning of all stories. We might put that in a much more boring way by saying that stories begin with a problem, a bother, a dilemma or a lack or yearning for something. Something isn't OK and our hero (of any kind, human or otherwise) wants to deal with it or has to deal with it.

I'm saying this because people often say to me that they would like to write. Of course it all depends on what you want to write. I'm starting off here with some kind of fiction: a story, film script, TV script, some kind of scenario for a dance or a musical.

I'm also saying it because one of the great ways to have a good day is to write. This may be through writing something that relates to feeling unhappy. I've found that I can write myself out of being unhappy by writing about … er … being unhappy! My person up a tree could be a version of me. Or it could be someone as far removed as I could possibly make them. That's great, because to write about them I must become absorbed in the problems I invent for them rather than in my own. That said, I can at any time weigh my character down with versions of what I'm feeling.

So let's stick with writing a fiction that isn't directly about me (or you!). The first step then is imagining and picturing the 'stuck up the tree' condition. It may well be a situation you know about from your family, relatives, friends or a news story. The next step is to explore it. Think about the whys and wherefores. How did this situation (up a tree) come about? What does the person think about it? Does that person blame others for it? Then we move into how we're going to get the person 'out of the tree'. Do they do it on their own? Do they seek help? Do they get help? If you want your story to keep people reading, we need tension, stress, a 'what happens next?' This means that we need obstacles. Where do these come from? Why is someone stopping our person getting out of the tree? Is it because they have some 'previous' with the person up the tree? If so, what?

Incidentally, you may well want more than one person stuck up the tree. Many 'situations' that are full of problems, bothers, dilemmas and the like, are shared by more than one person. In which case, the different ways in which those people handle the problem might well be what your story is all about. Do they help or hinder each other? Why?

You can do a lot of this without putting pen to paper. You can just play around with it in your mind. If it engages you, at some point the dam will break. You'll want to commit something and write it down. It's the writer's 'itch'. Whatever you're writing, you need the itch!

As you daydream and/or start to write, then we have so far missed out a key element in your vision: where is the 'tree'? That's to say, what and when is the setting? What timeframe are we in, and where are we? And remember, you have the whole of known history to play with, the whole of the known universe to play with, and you have any kind of imaginary place or time to play with, too. As your pen hovers over the page or your fingers over the keyboard, you might want to ask yourself why you have chosen this time and place! What's it going to give you? Danger? Absurdity? Corruption? Inequality? Hate? Desperation? Or what? You may well want and need plenty of that sort of thing because people like to read about characters facing problems.

All this is your platform for your story.

Now some principles:

Nothing can or should be solved simply. Or if a problem is solved simply, it should be an illusion. The character is deluding themselves that it's been solved. Problems need to be complicated on account of the character's foibles, past 'sins', weaknesses, secrets, etc., and/or complicated by who is the help or the hindrance. That's to say people come into a story with their own motives and agendas that complicate things. Good!

Throughout, whoever is speaking or doing things needs to have motives. You need to find motives for them. They must 'want' something. Your problem in the story will be to find out or ensure that they do or don't get what they want.

In a story, there may be one or more catalysts. These are people (or events bigger than the character like a war, a storm, a disaster, a plague, etc.) that make the 'cogs' of the story turn. The cogs are the ongoing actions: two people falling in love, or someone plotting against another – that sort of thing. A catalyst can help, hinder or divert the cogs. Who or what are your catalysts?

How or why do we care about characters? In good writing, we don't know why we care! The writer's job is to hide secret stores of information about the characters that help us know them. These can be bits of backstory about them. They can be confessional moments where we find out what the characters really think. They can be comments by others about a character. You can think of these as 'thickening' your character, giving them more substance. You can also hide these secret stores of information in telling us about what the character 'sees'. Your character walks into a room. What do they see? What do they not see? What do others notice about what your character sees?

All this raises the question that is pompously called 'interiority'. First issue: who is telling the story? Is it a 'he/she/it/they' story as noticed by the invisible narrator? Is it an 'I/we' story as noticed by a narrator who is part of the action? Or is it a 'multiple narration', told by different characters?

When you've got that sorted, you have to decide whether your narration can 'see' into one person's mind, or several people's minds. This reveals their thoughts, memories, imaginations and motives. You can write stories that can only 'see' one person's mind (just as in real life) and the character has to figure out what other people are thinking, just as you and I do, from the outside, through what they say and do. Or you can confine 'seeing' into the minds of just two people. Or you can have it so that the reader can see into the minds of anyone and everyone. It's up to you.

If you want people to read and enjoy your story, there have to be hooks. These are what's called 'reveal–conceal' (see also F is for Fiction). As you reveal, you have to conceal what's coming. In a way, writing a story is about writing a series of hints that aren't finished till we get to the end. There should always be something that isn't solved, that may or may not happen, that is still a question and is a tease for the reader – it should almost be annoying for them that they don't know yet. It's the opening line of *Hamlet*, which is 'Who's there?' The characters don't know. We don't know. And if the characters are sufficiently scared and mystified, then so will we be! Whatever intrigues or mystifies a character (who we care about) will intrigue or mystify a reader.

What about your style? Think of this as the voices you can use. Writing stories is about inventing and being someone or some people. These people need voices. Part of voice is style. And this applies to the outside narrator voice too. Take Dickens. He creates many different voices for his characters and then there's a Dickensian narrator's voice which is often jokily pompous, ironically making comments about the characters, often 'going on a bit'. You can find other narrations that are the opposite: clipped, spare, dry and 'getting on with it'. Or with, say, Hilary Mantel, unfolding the detail of places and the state of mind of characters as if the narrator is revealing an embroidered cloth.

Many writers will tell you that you should try out every sentence as if you're saying it out loud to a half-interested reader. You can't assume that they will stay in the room or even stay awake. Every sentence has to have something in it that they will want to hear. In that sense, writing is not about you, it's about them. Fix that half-interested person in your mind, and do everything you can to keep them awake.

Don't be proud. Use *Roget's Thesaurus*. That doesn't mean be fancy and wordy, just for the sake of it. It means keeping things fresh and various – which is also a way of keeping your reader awake! Find expressions that will delight and surprise.

Fill your story with traps, false leads, surprises, dashed hopes. Your readers are guessing ahead. You need to wrong-foot them. They will be glad to be wrong. Predictability has to be avoided.

At some point, you might want to ask, what are you saying with this story? And why? What are you saying about the human condition? And/or what are you saying about the human condition in this particular time and place – as with Hilary Mantel again?

If you're writing comedy, then you will find that humour comes from at least three sources: the narration, what the characters say and what the characters do. When it comes to what the characters do, you have a repertoire of tools like coincidence, embarrassment, disaster, absurdity, foolishness, 'kicking up' and 'kicking down' (in terms of mocking or demolishing others), parody, self-harm and so on. It helps to think of 'set pieces' when a set of characters come together in some kind of showdown – usually disastrous or absurd.

Finally, be a student! Study what other writers do. How did they make you care? How did they get you to be tense, scared, sorry, sad, sympathetic, unsympathetic? How did they mislead you? How did they 'take you to the place' of the action? How did they take you into the mind of the character?

Imitate but don't copy! What I mean is that we can imitate how they created these feelings but it's best to avoid copying the 'what', because readers will rumble it and the illusion will die.

So all this is about creating the artifice of a story about others. You might end up putting yourself in it. The important point is the gratification in doing it, or even the distraction of doing it. Then you might consider reading it or giving it to others. And this will lead to another whole set of challenges and potential pleasures. It may also guide you in what to write next. People might ask you to write 'something else like that'.

Oh yes, then you're flying.

Now for something completely different.

I've recently started doing a new kind of show. I read some poems (some might call them 'pieces') from a book called *Pebbles*. I say to the audience that while I'm reading they're free to write anything that comes into their heads. Then after I've read for about 40 minutes, I take a break, and encourage people to go on writing. After about another ten minutes or so, I say, 'Now we're going to have a pebbles show, made up of what you've written.' We pass the mic around and we have a brand-new poetry show created then and there.

This needs unpacking. The book is called *Pebbles* because the book is like a pebbly beach.

Each poem or piece in the book is very, very short and tweet-sized. They are a mix of things I've overheard, things

I've seen, observations about emotions, strange happenings, wishes, irritations, ironies, passing thoughts, memories, imaginings ... Some of them are trivial, some of them (even though I say so) significant, some just plain strange. As I explain in the intro, it's not that each 'pebble' is itself important. The way the book works is that the pebbles make the beach; the small pieces make up something that has meaning, according to one 'pebble' being next to another which is next to another which is next to another and so on. The aim of the evening is to create a beach out of the pebbles that the audience write. We move from profound to sad to absurd to nostalgic to hopeful to despair all in one sitting.

It's my view that this way of writing is just as much a representation of how we feel and think as a novel, a film, a single great poem or song. It's my view that we think in fragments. Quite often these are disjointed. And so they throw before us strange juxtapositions and comparisons. One moment we might be thinking of the time we fell in the river, the next a plan to deal with a bully at work, the next the look on your mother's face, the cat food that you're supposed to buy ... and so on. Mostly, writing doesn't grasp these kinds of rapid transitions. We think of good writing as being coherent, flowing in an orderly way from one sentence to the next, from one paragraph to the next. This kind of writing isn't interested in that. It just records the fragments as they arise in our minds.

The great advantage of this kind of writing is that it's easy to write a fragment. It's something you can see. It's something you just heard. It's something you just thought. It's something you just remembered. It's something you just hoped might happen. And so on.

All you have to do is jot it down and then – important, this – turn over the page and write another one when it occurs to you. There is no pressure to create a plot, no pressure to 'set' what you're writing in a time or place. There's no pressure to create characters. This is a very free and simple way of writing. You don't even have to write in sentences! It can be phrases or even single words. You can write lists, streams of thoughts, in any shape you want to. You don't have to write across a whole line as this book does. You can write one word a line, two words a line – whatever you want.

If you want to make some of it or all of it rhyme, then do it. If you don't want to, don't. It's up to you. Pebbles come in many different shapes. Make your own. Have fun.

My bed eats socks.
I go to bed with two socks on.
In the morning
I find that I have one sock on.
I look for the sock.
I can never find it.
My bed eats socks.

Final score
Arsenal 3 Chelsea 1
Chelsea won the second half (0–1) That's a fact.
But is it the whole truth?

There's something I should be doing and I'm not doing it.
It doesn't even matter any more what it is that I'm not doing.
All that's going on is a person not doing what they should be doing.

I

had

a

chocolate

Hobnob.

Two

actually.

I

had

two

chocolate

Hobnobs.

The

second

chocolate

Hobnob

was

as

good

as

the

first

chocolate

Hobnob.

If

not

better.

Why did they think that the mind and body are two different things? Apart from anything else you can see that they're joined together with what we call the neck.

There are times
when the only thing worth doing is to spear an olive.

SUGGESTION

Write pebbles.

Write anything.

Write on your phone.

Write in a beautiful notebook that you've bought specially for the purpose.

Write on the beach where you know the sea will wash it away.

Write.

X

is for X-ray

I was knocked over in the road.

When I came round, I was in hospital, with a sling round my middle suspending me from a bar above my bed. A doctor explained to me that I had 'broken' my pelvis but I hadn't broken any pelvic bones. What had happened was the impact of the car had wrenched apart my pelvis at the front. A few days later, they brought me an X-ray to look at. The doctor showed me how the two loops at the front of the pelvis had come apart and moved out of alignment. One loop was higher than the other.

I lay in bed staring at the image, fascinated by the idea that an X-ray could see inside me and show what had happened. I hold the image in my head more than 60 years later. I was 17.

What I liked then – and what I've liked ever since along with all the scans I've had – is that these inventions and machines can read inside us. I think of the millennia when the insides of living human beings were invisible. People divined what was going on or what had happened, using their sensitive touch on the outside, and studied urine, stools, saliva, eyes, skin, nails and teeth. Of course, when it was allowed, they looked inside dead bodies and tried to read what they saw spread out in front of them, too. In wars, medics of one kind or another had good sight of the battered and mangled bodies on the battle-field. They could look on bones, muscles, veins, arteries and organs torn, crushed, smashed and twitching. Insides became outsides. There must have been many moments of discovery in these terrible and terrifying circumstances as dying hearts pumped blood out onto the ground through severed arteries.

But, as I say, they couldn't see inside the living human body from the comfort – well, discomfort actually – of a hospital bed. Medics can stand around an X-ray and discuss the shadows and lines. As I lay in my sling, the doctor explained that there was nothing they could do with a pelvis that had been pulled apart other than to use my own weight pressing down on the sling to cause the sides of the sling to push my pelvis together and wait till it healed itself. Think of me lying in a small hammock, but instead of me lying in a hammock longwise, the hammock is under me crosswise. And I'm thinking every day about what it looks like inside me and how it's changing because somehow I'm sticking it back together again.

I know the word 'revelation' is charged with religious meaning, but this was a form of revelation. Again, many years later, I was at the dentist. We had moved so he was a 'new' dentist. He looked inside my mouth and gasped. He saw a set of molars filled with metal.

'I need to look at what's going on there,' he said, and set up X-rays for them.

When he looked at these he gasped again.

He swung my chair round and pointed at his light board.

'Look at that!' he said. 'It's some kind of screw!'

Sure enough, in this ancient repair job on my rear upper molar there was the outline of screw. It was as if someone had left it there by mistake. It was such an alien thing to be there and the thing is, it had been in there for about 55 years without me ever knowing it was there. The only thing I remember about the dental procedures from that time was that the dentist was a muscular, middle-aged, French Jewish woman who, it was said, fancied my dad and swore at me in French for misusing and abusing my teeth.

'Tu m'emmerdes, Michael!' (Meaning 'you annoy me' – although literally it has the sense of 'you shit me up'.)

As I looked at the screw, I imagined her armed with pliers and a screwdriver, driving the screw into my tooth. (In case you're wondering, I'm fairly sure it wasn't like that.)

It was both a revelation to see the screw but also a trigger taking me back to those times I sat in Madame's chair while she gripped me in a neck lock, swearing at me.

Teeth are intimate. We're checking them and licking them all day long. We know their inner edges so well. Dentists don't seem to care about this part of our teeth. Now, looking at the X-ray, I had a new knowledge about that rear molar.

One more: a year after my spell in hospital with Covid, I was asked to go to the 'brain hospital' for a scan. I lay in the tunnel and listened to the roar of the scanner, wondering what they would end up 'seeing'. What would they read?

Later, I was asked down into the basement of the hospital, where there was a large screen and a group of people sitting round it. The main brain doctor sat close to the screen, turned to me and said, 'Would you like to see your brain?'

Instantly, I thought of my work. A good deal of it involves me looking at my brain. Usually, I don't call it that. I call it 'wondering what's in my mind', or 'wondering what I thought about such-and-such'. But isn't that actually my brain? I know that huge books have been written about whether the mind is the brain but at that very moment, it really did feel as if the consultant was asking me if I wanted to see my mind. And I did. And I do. It sounded then, and it still does, like an adventure.

I said, yes.

He switched on the screen and there was what to my eyes looked like a cross-section through a cauliflower. The consultant seemed totally engaged with it, excited even.

'Your brain looks as if you've had altitude sickness,' he said and pointed at edges of the cauliflower florets.

I said that the highest I had been recently was the fourth floor of the Whittington Hospital. He stared some more.

'Should I be worried?' I said.

'No, no,' he said, 'you've done very well.'

I'm always bemused when doctors say that I've done very well when my body has done some healing of some kind. The man who did my electrocardiogram called out from other side of the room as my heart made noises like the bath emptying, 'Your left ventricular fraction has done very well.'

Suddenly I was proud of my left ventricular fraction and proud that I had done so well. What? I hadn't done anything, had I? It had done it itself.

Now the brain consultant was congratulating me, too. I accepted his praise with a modest glance down to the floor.

He then flicked through some more cross-sections of the cauliflower, nodding and smiling, occasionally pointing at frills and curves, and the other people nodded and smiled too. I could almost have thought that they were reading my mind. And then I thought, *Hey, when they made this scan that I'm looking at, I was thinking. That's a photo of a thought. But what was I thinking?* I remembered that when the scanner roared, I thought of being in the London Underground. Yes, that is a photo of me thinking about the London Underground. I went on thinking. What if there will be a time when scanners can read your thoughts? Secret police would get hold of you and scan your brain in prison. And then … I pondered on … they would lie to you and tell you that you were planning to blow up the

Houses of Parliament when in actual fact you were thinking that you really would like some hummus to eat.

The brain consultant could see that I was daydreaming.

'So, all good, Mr Rosen,' he said, 'you won't need to come back.'

Disappointing. I really would have liked to come back and see my brain again.

'Do you want to know the results of the cognitive reasoning test we gave you?'

'Yes.'

'Superior,' he said.

'I suppose you could tell that by looking at the scan,' I said.

I didn't say that. I've made that bit up.

I went home and told people that I had seen my brain and my cognitive reasoning was superior. I was very proud of this for a while but then I went online and found out that there was a category above superior so I've stopped going on about that now.

But I am still in a state of bliss about these revelations.

They remind me of near-ecstatic moments when I've discovered something or that something has suddenly become clear. Or when something that has been hidden for many years suddenly comes to light. Of course this last kind of revelation depends on other people but the feeling can be just as dramatic. Maybe, when we work hard at the first kind, after long months or years of digging, then the second kind just turn up.

Let me give you some examples.

As you may know (because I've written about it), I tried for years to find out what had happened to my father's French uncles. All I knew was, in his words, that 'they were there before the war and they weren't there after the war'. He knew their names – Oscar and Martin. He said that he thought one was a dentist and one was a clock-mender and that they had lived in the cities on east side of France. The end. That was it.

It frustrated me enormously because it seemed to me that there was a Hitlerian double victory here: they had been exterminated according to the plan, but also all trace of them had disappeared – also part of the plan, as they (and we) were supposed to be an 'extinct race'. No matter where or how I looked I couldn't find Oscar and Martin Rosen – not even on the huge list, compiled so diligently and carefully by the Holocaust historian Serge Klarsfeld. How could two people just disappear?

And then, out of the blue, in the files of the recently deceased brother of the mother of my second cousin (!), four letters were found. Two were from Oscar Rosen, and two from Stella Rosen in Poland, the mother of the sole surviving 'continental' Rosens in my family.

This was the X-ray moment. A revelation. Now I had addresses. Once again, my digging got going, and I was soon ordering up books and archives from France. As each book and document arrived, I could piece together another part of the journey my father's uncles made from their homes in Sedan and Metz (on the east side of France, as my father had remembered), to the west side of France and then in their different ways on trains ('convoys') to Auschwitz.

My family, no doubt, are witness to the many times I made eureka noises as another part of the story came clear.

'Look at this,' I said to them, when the archive of the '*département*' (like a county) of Vendée came back with the arrest report of my father's uncle Martin. I sat staring at the writing of the 'adjutant' as he related to his superiors that he had arrested Martin Rozen (Polish spelling) at 2.30 in the morning of 31 January 1944 from the house of Mme Bobières in the village of Sainte-Hermine. I read the descriptions of his height, hair colour, eye colour, his shoes, his jacket, his trousers, the scar on his cheek, the beret he wore. The report was co-signed by three other policemen. It tells how the police handed over Martin to the authorities in the nearby town of La Roche-sur-Yon.

In a single two-page, handwritten document was a major part of the history of the Holocaust: the orderly and 'legal' arrest of someone who had done nothing illegal, his transfer from one group of the justice system to another, one form of custody to another, until this person arrived at a place where they would be killed.

I often think how I might never have found this document. I might never have dug it out, made it known to my family or to anyone else. I might never have been able to reveal it. I might never have known that this was what happened to people (my grandfather's generation) who were once brothers and sisters in Poland.

I thought of how that generation made choices, some to stay in Poland, some to emigrate to France, some to emigrate to London, some to the US. For each of them there was a different fate depending on decisions made far away by governments and generals, just as the poet Matthew Arnold described, some 90 years before:

And we are here as on a darkling plain
Swept with confused alarms of struggle and flight,
Where ignorant armies clash by night.

('Dover Beach', published in 1867,
probably written in 1851)

And that's a revelation in itself. How amazing that a rather stern and sober Victorian could have described (revealed?) something full of a meaning and feeling that tells a tale that happened so many years later to people in my family!

Maybe my interest in X-rays and scans is a literary one. Not fully known to me, I want X-rays and scans to do the same job as poems and stories. And vice versa. I want poems and stories to do the same job as X-rays and scans: to reveal what we couldn't see before.

SUGGESTION

What happens if you X-ray any part of your life, or any part of your mind?

If, for a moment, you imagine there is, as with your body and X-rays, a hard distinction between what you can see and what lies behind it, or in it, what can you find under the surface, out of sight?

Take one example: your mother is talking to you. You can 'see' her face in your mind. It's at some 'crunch' moment.

Now X-ray it.

What do you think she is thinking? Why?

What are you thinking? Why?

Is there anyone else in the room or in this place?

X-ray them. What are they thinking?

Now you have that power, what happens if you apply it to other people and other situations? Make a list of them.

Plan your next X-rays.

Write them down.

Y

is for Youth

This may seem strange, but it's taken me years to figure out that there's not really a lot of difference between my late son's childhood and my other children's childhoods. They're all in the past – equally so. Mine too. I have to admit that for many years, when I thought about my late son's childhood, it often made me deeply, deeply sad. I'd think about standing with him on the terraces at Highbury (Arsenal's former stadium), taking him to play hockey and watching him kitted out in huge pads playing in goal, playing the 'how do we get home' game in which we came up with fantastical ways of turning ourselves into other creatures which could, say, be so small that we could whizz through the telephone wires that you used to see by the side of railway lines, listening to him telling his jokes and how he brought me the play he wrote just a few weeks before he died, and on and on. There were times when I didn't want to think about these things. It felt like the hole in your mouth after you've had a tooth pulled.

Then one day, and it really was as sudden as this, I was thinking about the way he used to make up plays with his stepsister, and I thought, *What's the difference between the two of them?* I've touched on this already in D is for Death but let me explain it again here. Both those childhoods are past. I can't 'have' them or be 'in' either of them. My stepdaughter is alive. Eddie isn't. But I can be no more in the past of one than the other. They exist as memories of both of them – however it is that we do the incredible thing of storing the things that happen to us. It's not as if the memory of Eddie's stepsister is more available or more get-at-able. I concede there is one difference in that I can have a conversation with Eddie's stepsister about those plays, but it's quite possible that she doesn't remember much about them.

Perhaps this is obvious to you, but it was a moment of discovery for me and it led to more thinking about childhood and youth. Traditionally, in the culture I've grown up in, memories of youth are tinged with sadness, nostalgia and regret. People openly express how sorry they are that they're not young any more or that things aren't as good now as they were 'then'. When people reminisce – and I'm a reminiscence addict – it often drifts downwards into a sense of loss. The most obvious reason for this is that we have lost our youth. In fact, I often meet teenagers who express something very similar about their 'childhoods'. They come towards me with their battered copies of *We're Going on a Bear Hunt* and say things like 'You were my childhood', or 'We used to sing this in the car when we were on holiday'. By the age of 13 or 14, they often talk in terms of having lost something that was special or valuable that they can't get back.

Apart from anything else, figuring this out has helped me cope with the fact that I've lost Eddie's childhood. But more than that: it's helped me think about all my children's childhoods and, indeed, my own. I tell myself: I need to find a way to wholeheartedly accept that these events and feelings have passed. After all, if I remember them, they're not really 'lost', are they? The real lost memories aren't memories. You know the moment, when you meet someone and they start telling you about the time you and they were sent to the head-teacher's room for flicking ping-pong balls in assembly and you have no memory of it … or some such. So a memory of childhood and youth, no matter how horrible, is in essence ours. We can say, 'It's mine. It's part of who I am. It's part of what's made me.'

Where does this get me? It takes me to thinking that there really is no point in regretting that those childhood things are past. That is as much a part of our lives as human beings as breathing. We have pasts. The moment before this moment is past. The moment when I was three, 75 years ago, and sitting on the beach at Margate is past. (It was very hot and I didn't like sand. I thought sand was a very bad idea.)

There's more: for anyone reading this who's over the age of, let's say, 35, there are already things that you could do when you were younger that you can't do as easily now. Anyone who follows sport knows that somewhere between 35 and 40 most sportspeople have to accept that they can't do things as fast or as strongly or as often as they could when they were younger. (If 35 seems too young a high-tide mark, think of the foot-baller Ronaldo or the tennis player Novak Djokovic – even they know that by 40, things are changing!) For those of us who don't spend hours and hours every day training, these tail-offs are more marked. Obviously. So again, small wonder that the youthful past seems like a better place.

I have a strange illness called hypothyroidism. When it's not treated, we hypothyroid sufferers become incapacitated in many different ways. In theory, the treatment solves this. In practice, it often doesn't. Doctors try to balance out our dosages of the replacement therapy so that we are 'normal'. As I'm writing this, I'm fully aware that my dosage was reduced a few months ago, and I'm just as aware that some of those symptoms – like having heavy legs when going upstairs, getting cramps in my muscles when I do repetitive movements – have come back. And guess what? It makes me fed up! And guess what? It makes me think of when I was 15 and going running, or when I was 18 and playing rugby ... Disastrous thing to do!

I'm back with the hopeless harking-back that I used to do with Eddie's childhood. I can't bring my youthful moments back. I can't reinhabit them. I can't be in them. So not only do I have to accept that the past is a place I can't revisit, but also that I must therefore think, think and think of the present. And it's true, the only way I can be genuinely happy is to do something now. Ironic bit coming up: this is true, even if the way I'm happy is to think about the past! You may or may not know but a major part of my job is to talk to people of any age about the past. And that makes me happy.

So Y is for Youth is not about forgetting or regretting. I tell myself that there's no point in trying to forget the past – it never works. I can always regret the past, but at some point I have to accept that the past happened, just as leaves go brown in autumn.

One reason why all this is so difficult – at least I for one find it difficult to think through and understand – is because of how youth and childhood are 'constructed'. This is an odd idea because surely being a child and being young just happen. No one constructs them, surely? That's a theory in itself. If we say childhood just is childhood then that's a theory that there is some kind of permanent state of being that lives across history and across continents that IS childhood.

Let's test this. On the radio as I was writing this book, there was a news item about the huge market in make-up for primary-school-age girls. This is make-up that they wear. I was at primary school in north London from 1950 to 1957. I heard of girls experimenting with their mother's make-up in the bathroom at home, but never wearing it in public to, say, a school social event or at parties at the weekend. This is one tiny glimpse of how childhood is redefined and recreated across time and place.

Some more examples: my teenage years came just after the decade in which the teenager had been invented as a category that could be targeted as a mass market and as a type. I landed in a world already inhabited by Little Richard, Elvis, Brenda Lee, jeans, T-shirts, slicked-back hair and a hundred other 'markers' of what a teenager should do or be. The teens in the West, in, say, the nineteenth century, spent much more of their lives either carrying on with childhood or pressed into the adulthood of work. The word 'teenager' itself doesn't seem to have appeared until around 1912.

Another way to trace how childhood and youth are constructed is to look at how adults wrote for children and young people. We take it for granted that though books for children can be 'tough' or 'face up to problems', there is an overall assumption that children's books are 'innocent' and that no matter what difficulties the children in the books face, things will work out well in the end. We are so used to this being the way things are, we hardly notice it. But were books for children always like this? In fact, we can ask, were there always books for children, because even the idea of there being a separate space for a child to think of themselves going through adventures had to be invented?

If we go back to Tudor times in England, say, you'd be hard pushed to find any kind of book that was for children that resembled anything like the children's books of today in which children talk, act and think about the world they're in. Whatever books that were put deliberately in front of children were about instructing them how to read or teaching them aspects of Christianity. At the same time, there's plenty of evidence that children got hold of adventures through 'street literature', the ballads and song-sheets that were sold on the streets, in markets and fairs and the like. These were stories of fantastical things like giant fish, or there were 'murder ballads', 'romances' and adventures. But, importantly, these weren't directed specifically at children, with child heroes at the centre of them.

There were simple stories of Aesop's Fables available but, again, the characters in those stories are talking animals representing 'types' of behaviour, not direct representations of children. The first time children become the centrepieces of narratives and books is with a genre of story that to our ears seems very strange. They are sad tales of babies and young children dying before they were baptised. In the minds of those who wrote these was the 'fact' that such children would go to Hell, as they were born with 'original sin', as inherited from 'man's fall' in the Garden of Eden. I realise that this is a lot to take in in one sentence! The point is that some of the first people to create stories for children, and indeed to 'notice' them at all, felt duty-bound to save children from the terrible fate of going to Hell. To be clear, this wasn't because these babies and young children had done bad things, but that they were born bad, as we all are. If you can bear to read these books, they don't resemble anything like the books we give children today. In fact, you wouldn't be allowed to put such books in front of children today!

Clearly, then, for those who gave children such books, they were 'constructing' childhood in a very different way from the way we do, or even from the way that the early nineteenth-century writers did. Something must have happened between the time when it was thought children were born bad and the time when it was thought that children were innocent.

In the late seventeenth and early eighteenth centuries, a movement grew which put forward the idea that children learned about the world through their senses and not through being beaten. It was claimed that sensing things came before understanding things. To read these ideas feels as though 'the child' has been pulled out of the great universal system of sin and redemption into a world in which 'the child' as an individual, plays, discovers and learns. Just to be clear, these ideas weren't universally accepted and they still aren't! The point I'm making is that these ideas began to circulate around Europe and started to affect how children were viewed.

The background reason for this new view of childhood is that a new class of people was emerging in Europe that was pushing at the privilege and autocratic rule of the aristocracy.

The aristocracy had owed its position to birth and breeding. The new class needed ideas to justify why they could have power and control in society. What better way to instil that confidence than to start with children showing them they could go out and look at the world, sense it, and then understand it! The aristocracy didn't need to do that, because they owned the world.

One more twist to this story: by the time the Romantics came along (late eighteenth and into the nineteenth century), the child and the young person were put at the centre of things even more. William Wordsworth said the 'child is the father to the man', meaning that we adults, who are spoiled by the ways of the world ('getting and spending'), should learn from the way children 'wonder' about the world. It was two poets who were part of the wider Romantic movement, Jane and Ann Taylor, who wrote 'Twinkle twinkle little star, how I WONDER what you are ...' By the end of the nineteenth century, a popular form of children's literature consisted of novels in which good children redeem 'fallen' parents.

In that short outline, we can see that a lot of work goes into 'constructing' childhood and that it changes over time.

This means that whatever feelings we have about our childhood and teenage years, these feelings can't be disentangled from the constructions we inherit and are part of. We might genuinely feel that when we were, say, ten years old, we were 'innocent'. Or that when we were in our teens, we were 'free'. Even so, I find it refreshing to challenge myself about such things. When I was ten, was I innocent? Quite simply, without going into details, I was not. When I was a teen, was I 'free'? No. In terms of power and control, of course my parents were totally in charge, apart from a few hours in school where school was in charge. And yet I can 'feel' as if I were an innocent child and a free teen. There's a contradiction between what I know to be true and what I feel. I'm suggesting that that's because I'm entangled with what are called 'prevailing' ideas about childhood and youth, even though I might carry opposite thoughts in my mind.

At the end of the day, this is about dispelling unhappiness, regret and loss. I don't mean 'shy away from'. It's more to do with finding peace of mind in 'placing' this stuff where it makes sense.

SUGGESTION

Your youth is yours. Even though it's gone, you still have it in your mind. Can you come up with a worst bits/best bits list when you think about it?

(More lists.)

Now see if you can remember when people (parents, teachers, youth group leaders, radio, newspaper, TV) seemed to be saying to you what kind of child they wanted you to be? What did they mean when they said they wanted you to be 'good'?

What did 'naughty' or 'bad' mean? What was 'bad behaviour' or a 'bad way to be'?

How did they express that?

So now you're an adult, where does the good child and the bad child sit in you?

Are you still sometimes the good child and sometimes the bad child? Is that funny or sad or awkward or painful?

Why's that?

I think that thinking about these things helps me join my adulthood to my childhood. It helps me avoid being 'fractured'. Pulls it all together. And it often joins up the good days of the past with the good days of now.

Z

is for Zephaniah and Zimmerman
(Benjamin Zephaniah and Robert Zimmerman, Bob Dylan)

I've spent many happy hours with my mind filled with the thoughts and sounds of these two Zs. In their different ways, they are people who I've thought of as clever and wise and above all else, able to say things through their poetry, music and comments that have got me thinking and feeling good. We need that, don't we? Some people call it 'escape' but I don't go with that. I think of it more like going into a room and finding someone you want to listen to. It's not an escape because you might find yourself in what they're saying, or you might find moods and worlds that you had never thought of before. That's often been the case with Benjamin Z and Bob Z.

I'm know that I'm alive at a time that wants to mix such pleasures with words like 'genius', 'hero', 'guru', 'fan', 'hero-worship', 'adulation' or 'cult'. I'm mildly irritated by this. I don't want to be part of something that involves me surrendering myself to my Zs. The challenge for me is how to admire and enjoy them and have my mind working, without losing myself.

I'll start with Dylan. As with a lot of our attachments to figures in the arts, there was a moment when it seemed as if something both original and perfectly formed had landed from outer space. Of course, the truth was neither of those things. He was a musician who in his own special way had studied hard how to write, sing and play. And he wasn't from outer space: he was from the mid-West and had migrated to New York City. Hearing about these things and remembering them was just one way of many in which I could, and still do, enjoy the reality of the person. There was another link: before I heard Dylan, I had spent many a good hour listening to Woody Guthrie, Dylan's first 'master'. Sixty years before the film *A Complete Unknown* came out, I was hearing how Dylan had visited Guthrie in hospital where he was suffering from a ghastly debilitating illness, Huntington's chorea. I was moved by the idea of someone new emerging from an apprenticeship, a laying on of hands with a musician that I already loved and admired.

When I first heard Dylan's album *The Freewheelin' Bob Dylan*, when I was 17 or 18, the songs seemed to think what I wanted to think. How come a song could anticipate my thoughts and feelings? It helped that I felt that I was already part of the musical world that Dylan had landed in in New York. One of my Guthrie albums combined Guthrie with Brownie McGhee, Sonny Terry and Cisco Houston, so the sound of a harmonica over guitar was in my bloodstream. I went out and bought a harmonica.

Some of the songs on *The Freewheelin' Bob Dylan* are full of mysterious phrases. When he wrote and sang songs that were like folk songs, the roots showed. The more mysterious songs seemed like a mix of the biblical and the Beat Poets – Allen Ginsberg in particular – who had their special place in the right-hand pocket of my school blazer. How was he mixing this stuff up and putting it together into songs? Many years later, Joan Baez told us about 'scruffy little Bob' voraciously reading anything he could lay his hands on, and then scribbling away for hours on end. That makes sense. I love the idea that a writer can be a blender. The writer pours piles of different ingredients in, switches it on and out comes a great soup. The critic Christopher Ricks pieced together that T.S. Eliot was doing something similar when he wrote the great poem 'The Love Song of J. Alfred Prufock', so this idea that you could grab phrases, make allusions, jump from one concept to another, mixing and mashing resonant images had been about for several decades before Bob arrived. T.S. Eliot stared out from the photos and chanted mournfully (as you can hear, on recordings), while Dylan's voice pleaded and cajoled over a guitar being played like Bluegrass and Blues musicians. There were people who said his voice was 'whiney'. What I could hear was the sound of Guthrie mixed in with the 'mountain' singers I loved who sang through their noses about lost love and murder.

I saw Dylan at the Royal Albert Hall just at the moment before he went electric. He was still singing some of the folk and 'protest' material but in this concert he tried out 'It's Alright, Ma (I'm Only Bleeding)'. What the hell was this song? It wasn't and isn't either 'folk' or 'electric'. It felt at that moment entirely its own thing, with its mishmash of glittering images and political aphorisms, which, as I know now, have been quoted ever since. The backing from his acoustic guitar was more like rhythm guitar, his voice sounded like a reluctant guest explaining why he doesn't want to stay at the party. The 'only' in the title ('only dying') flagged up that the tone is cynical and ironic. Yes! Cynical and ironic was good. Very good. The memory has lasted.

Then he went electric. As a leftie folkie, I should have been as outraged as Pete Seeger and Alan Lomax – which we see in the recent film. My reaction was different. Alongside my leftie folkie leanings, I was also a fan of Chicago rhythm 'n' blues and the rock blues of Chuck Berry and Little Richard, as were, of course, the Beatles and the Stones. So my first thought when I heard Dylan go electric wasn't that he had 'betrayed' the 'purity' of the folk-protest song, but that he wasn't as good as Chuck Berry! I said to myself, if you're going to do this stuff, then why not be as good as them? (You see how I'm not a hero-worshipper.) I think I've figured out what I was doing there. I had compartmentalised my tastes into folky stuff over there, electric over here, such that I couldn't see that the endlessly restless Dylan had crossed over in order to make something new in the electric world. Another great thing about Dylan is that you can never catch up with him.

I nearly caught up by the time *Highway 61 Revisited* came out but not quite. Upstairs in our student flat, my flatmate Don was wearing out his copy of the album. He played one side, he turned it over, played that side, turned it over, played the first side, turned it over ... on and on. I became just as interested in why Don was playing it as I was in the album. What was he gripped by? What was it doing for him?

When I listened, I thought that this band was good. But what was he singing about? A question that has eaten up listeners and critics of Dylan before, then and ever since. Who are the people in 'Just Like Tom Thumb's Blues'? And why did it matter so much that he was just like a rolling stone?

I like it that I was behind the wheel – way, way behind the wheel, actually. It fluffs up the texture of what I think now. Our tastes evolve but I find it funny that here was an album that many musicians at the time saw straight away was something amazing and special, and yet at that moment I just thought it was 'interesting'.

I realise that if Dylan is of no interest to you, then the substance of what I'm saying here has little meaning. What I'm trying to express is that we can find such deep pleasures through immersing ourselves in the sounds, poetry and lives of people like Dylan. We don't have to get hung up on whether this or that is perfect or, as I say, whether he or she is a genius. The joy is in finding what we find.

I did see Bob in around 2000 but it didn't do it for me. He didn't seem to be enjoying himself, the songs or the band. He was being extra growly. I know that that's how he is these days but I didn't get it. No worries. I can sit in the dark at midnight and play hours of YouTube Bob I like. It's a great way to close a day. In one interview I saw, it's clear that even he is amazed by the way he wrote in the past. He quotes himself from 'It's Alright, Ma (I'm Only Bleeding)', and says that he can't write like that any more. As he says it, he looks puzzled. I like that.

I was puzzled by his song 'Gotta Serve Somebody'. At this point, Bob had become a believer. The surface idea in the song is that he is telling us that whether you're rich or poor, you've either got to serve the Devil or serve the Lord. It's a very symmetrical song, weighing up one kind of person against another, again and again, and then repeatedly coming back to the chorus where he talks about either the Devil or the Lord. Now, I'm not a believer, but unlike John Lennon, who took exception to the song, I like two things about it – on the one hand, there's the structure of it (which I've just described), but on the other, I don't have to take 'Devil' and 'Lord' literally. I can take 'Devil' to mean 'evil ends' and 'Lord' to mean 'good ends'. In which case, the song is talking about how you can be rich or poor, but one way or another you'll find yourself doing good things or bad. It's as if he's saying we all face an existential choice – what's it going to be? I've watched Dylan performing the song on YouTube and one strange thing about it is that every now and then there's a smile in his eyes. Is that because the audience he's singing to in the video that I keep watching is made up of multi-millionaire film and music stars?

While I was figuring this out, a request came in from the organisation that manages NHS Charities. Could I write and perform a poem for the Day of Reflection marking the fifth anniversary of when the Covid pandemic started in March 2020? I received a set of bullet points that the organisers hoped that I would hit. Hundreds of images came into my head from 2020, some to do with me, some to do with the health workers who saved my life, some to do with lockdowns. I thought of the way this Dylan song wasn't the kind where he seems to be throwing countless images at his audience. It was plain and direct. The power comes from the binary choices he gives us and the repeated binary in the chorus. Because the surface ideas of the song are Christian, I found myself thinking of the Litany in the *Book of Common Prayer* that has several different repeated lines – as with, for example, 'Good Lord, deliver us', which is repeated in chorus by the congregation. It's the classic 'call-and-response' form, at the heart of popular and religious culture for hundreds of years. I pictured myself standing at a lectern at this secular service to commemorate this hugely significant and complex year, 2020. One way I was familiar with this Litany was through a satire that was based on it, by the great satirist William Hone. Reading a parody can sometimes free you up to play with the original parodied text too.

Thanks to Dylan and William Hone, it came to me that I could create a call-and-response form, offering binaries, in order to build up how we felt about 2020. The choral response would be 'we remember' and I got down to writing the images. On 9 March 2025, I performed it at the National Memorial Arboretum to an invited audience of bereaved people, health workers and people who had been seriously ill. I asked people to join in with 'we remember', so that it was like a non-religious prayer.

Coughing and coughing, gasping for air
we remember
Empty streets, no cars anywhere
we remember
Curry with no flavour, pizza with no taste
we remember
Empty days, time to waste
we remember
Running out of tests and masks
we remember
What is this Zoom thing? someone asks
we remember
How many feet are we standing apart?
we remember
A pain in the chest, a pain in the heart
we remember

Children in their rooms all day
we remember
Will we never get away?
we remember
The unprotected driver of the bus
we remember
Nurses checking, testing us
we remember
Nurses wearing clinical waste bags
we remember
People leaving without their name tags
we remember
Freezing cold then helplessly hot
we remember
Blood thinners and blood clots
we remember
The face we'll never see again
we remember
A mind chasing grief and pain
we remember
The risks you took for working on and on
we remember
The fatigue and strain have never gone
we remember
The wards too hot in the June weather
we remember
Medics in teams, working together
we remember
The endless beeps of drips and machines
we remember
The news that they'd invented a vaccine
we remember
Those we met, the paths we crossed
we remember

Those who went, those we lost
we remember
The lives of those who fell or faltered
we remember
The lives of those forever altered
we remember

Along with all the thanks I owe to those who saved my life, there's a thanks for Robert Zimmerman for helping me say something that suited the occasion of a day of reflection about the Covid pandemic.

My other Z is Benjamin Zephaniah. I can't ignore the fact that what I say now is affected by the fact that he isn't here any more. I knew Benjamin. We kept bumping into each other in very different kinds of places: one time he was compering an awards ceremony for digital foreign language apps. Calm, wry, amused that it was him doing it. After all, he explained, he left school barely able to read and write and here he was giving out awards at a ceremony devoted to literacy. Another time it was on a vigil in support of someone held in custody because we were at war. Each time he would drop something that would set me thinking. On one occasion I asked him how he managed to stay so calm and clear when he appeared on BBC TV's *Question Time*. I said that I had been asked to go on several times, but I wasn't confident enough that I could say what I wanted to say as clearly as he does. So I refused. I was envious of how he seemed to find it so easy. And how come he could make topics clear that everyone else on the panel was making sound complicated? I asked him, how do you do it? And you always give examples or neat analogies. He said that he speaks as if he was talking to his mother. I knew his mother had been a nurse. She had come here from Jamaica and raised eight children. The first time I saw Benjamin perform he had danced a poem about his mother. There was something infectious about a man doing a dance about 'I love me mother and me mother loves me'. It's been an earworm ever since.

Question Time isn't the House of Commons. It isn't a university common room. It's a popular TV programme where, if you don't make things clear, you flap and flounder, and flannel comes out of your mouth. If you were at home blathering on and on like that, much as your mum might love you, she would probably switch off. I realised in that moment that I didn't have a mother whom I could reference. My mother was long gone, and the kind of political chat that I would get into with friends was weighed down by ifs and buts and 'on the other hands' – guaranteed to be hesitant and boring.

Two of us, Annemarie Young and I, put together a book about refugees and migrants for school students. I got in touch with Benjamin to ask him a few questions for a page in the book. He said that the way he saw it was that anyone could end up being a refugee. Things could change, governments, invasions, climate. He said that he took in some refugees once. Thinking that maybe they had come from Syria or Sudan, I asked him where were they from? The Lake District, he said. There were floods. They couldn't stay in their home so he took them in.

He put his passion and anger into poems as well as anyone I know but he kept it tight and controlled. He didn't hold back from saying what he wanted to say to young audiences. In the poem 'People Need People', he's complex and radical in direct ways. In the poem (and video) 'Rong Radio Station', the medium of the anger is irony. I once asked him where he wrote these poems. He said, 'How do you mean "write"?'

I said, 'Y'know, write, write your poems.'

He said, 'I don't write my poems.'

I thought, *He doesn't write his poems? Who does write his poems then? Or does he feel, maybe, that the poems write themselves? Or that he hears them and they speak to him?*

I said, 'You don't write your poems?'

'No,' he said, 'I make them up in my head when I go for a run. That way, when I get to the end of my run, I know them off by heart.'

A few months later, I was with some children by the River Thames in London. We had just been doing a poetry workshop in one of the rooms in the Southbank Centre. The children were going back to school and we all found ourselves under an arch of a railway bridge going over the Thames. As children do, the moment a train roared over their heads, they screamed. (Why do they always do this? Is it written down in some sacred text: 'When a train comes over a bridge and you're under it, thou shalt scream'?)

Something twigged in my mind, that maybe there was something else they could do, apart from screaming, so I said, 'Hey, I know we can all hear the train, but I wonder if you can feeeeel the train.' And I put my hands on the brick wall holding up the bridge. At that, they all put their hands on the wall.

So 30 children, their teachers, their teaching assistants and me all stood with our hands on the wall waiting for the next train. Sure enough, when it came, we felt the rhythm of the train.

And this is what I tell nearly every audience of children I meet: the moment I thought of this idea, I heard it as a possible beginning of a poem. And the moment I thought that, I also thought of the late, great Benjamin Zephaniah and what he said about making up poems in his head when he goes for a run. So I set myself the Benjamin Zephaniah Challenge: could I make up a poem in my head, so that I'd know it off by heart when I got to the end?

So that's what I did. I didn't actually go for a run. (There's a surprise.) I got on the London Underground – 'the Tube'. I sat there playing with the words, doing gestures to do with 'Hands on the …' It must have looked quite strange to see me muttering to myself, waving my hands about, smiling when I thought I had got a bit right. Anyway, by the end of the journey, I had a poem. I wanted it to have something of Benjamin about it, how he says things about life, in ways that are catchy and simple. I thought of how we are connected to each other, connected to our bodies, connected to the things we do, connected to the things we make or write – the kind of thing that Benjamin thought and wrote about. And it came out like this:

Hands on the bridge, feel the rhythm of the train.
Hands on the window, feel the rhythm of the rain.
Hands on your throat, feel the rhythm of your talk.
Hands on your legs, feel the rhythm of your walk.
Hands in the sea, feel the rhythm of the tide.
Hands on your heart, feel the rhythm inside.
Hands on the rhythm, feel the rhythm of the rhyme.
Hands on your life, feel the rhythm of time.

'Now then,' I say, as I go on talking to the children, 'Benjamin said something else. He said that if you make up a poem in your head, it comes out in a shape that is easy for people to learn. So here is Benjamin Zephaniah Challenge, number 2: do you think you could learn it?'

I then teach it to the children line by line, and we finish by doing it all in one go, together. They do. They really do. They know the poem. And at the end we give a huge cheer for the late, great Benjamin Zephaniah. It feels good. In fact, it feels like a good day.

Thank you Zs.

So I've finished with heroes. For me, heroes are not perfect. No one's perfect. They're heroes because they inspire me and help me have good times.

But more than that. Both Benjamin and Dylan are out-there people. Benjamin shared what he thought and wrote. He found that people wanted to hear that. He was also a great listener. Since he died, I've heard countless stories of how he listened to people, helped them, offered them advice, helped people express themselves. I don't know Dylan but he's a very paradoxical figure in that he has been touring and singing and talking on and off since he was about 13! (He was in a high school band.) When he introduces songs he is often quite obscure and elliptical. I keep getting the impression that he wants us to 'get' what he's on about without having to explain very much – or anything at all!

All these things to do with Benjamin or Dylan are about ways of talking, ways of making contact, ways of sharing, ways of being connected. That's all we've got. No matter how private we are (and a lot of this book has seemingly been about personal stuff), it only makes sense when we remember that it's all about being with other people. As Benjamin says, 'People need people.'

If at any point we think that people don't need people, terrible things start happening. In fact, the only way to stop such things happening is to find what it is we need from each other, what we can do with each other and what we can do for each other.

Which takes us back to old John Donne. There he sits, like a beacon, like a shining light, reminding any of us who care to be reminded that 'no man is an island'. (We'll have to forgive him that he restricted it to 'men'.)

SUGGESTION

What ways have you *not* been an island in your life?
What ways today are you not an island?
What ways tomorrow will you be not an island?